W9-CCF-236

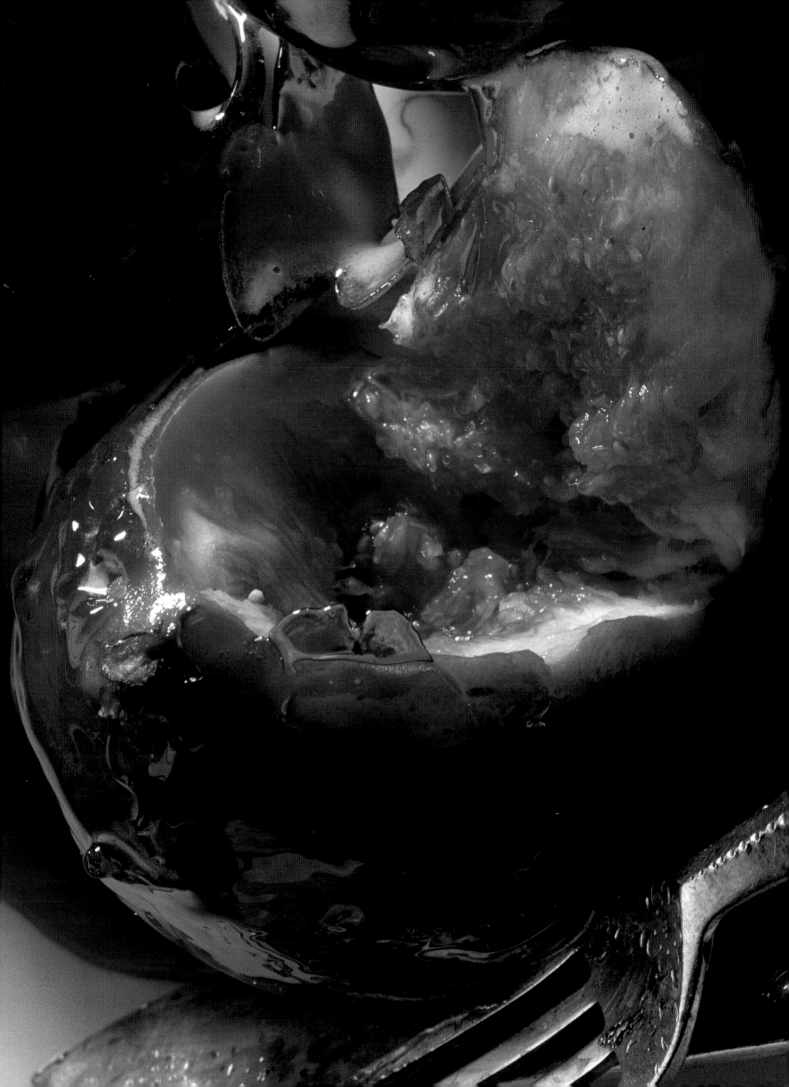

DESSERT
The Grand Finale

SEDGEWOOD® PRESS

US Edition published by
Sedgewood® Press
150 East 52nd Street
New York, NY 10022

Sedgewood® Press is an imprint of Meredith® Books:
President, Book Group: Joseph J. Ward
Vice President, Editorial Director: Elizabeth P. Rice

For Sedgewood® Press:
Executive Editor: Maryanne Bannon
Senior Editor: Carol Spier
Associate Editor: Guido Anderau
Associate Editor, Copywriter: Ruth Weadock

Produced by Weldon Russell Pty Ltd
107 Union Street
North Sydney
NSW 2060, Australia

Publisher: Elaine Russell
Publishing Manager: Susan Hurley
Editor: Kayte Nunn
Editorial Assistant: Libby Frederico
Author: Suzie Smith
Introduction: Kirsty McKenzie
Designer: Fred Rainey/Folio Art & Design
Food Stylist: Suzie Smith
Photographer: Joe Filshie
U.S. Cooking Consultant : Mardee Haidin Regan
Production: Dianne Leddy

© Weldon Russell Pty Ltd 1993

All rights reserved. No part of this publication may be
reproduced, stored in a retrieval system, or transmitted
in any form or by any means, electronic, mechanical,
photocopying, recording or otherwise, without the
prior written permission of the Publishers and the
copyright owner.

Address correspondence to Sedgewood® Press

Library of Congress number: 93-084587

ISBN: 0-696-02550-7

Distributed by Meredith Corporation
Des Moines, Iowa

Production by South China Printing
Printed in Hong Kong

A KEVIN WELDON PRODUCTION

C O N T E N T S

•

Prelude

•

Music may be the food of love, but true romantics the world over will testify that dessert is cupid's edible accompaniment. With its sweet notes of self-indulgence, forbidden elements and even aphrodisiac qualities, a meal's last course has grown to be regarded as an enhancer of the sweetness of love. And for range and complexity, there's a whole orchestra of options for the meal's finale.

he word "dessert" comes from the French verb *desservir* (to remove that which has been served) and refers to all foods offered to guests after the previous dishes and their utensils have been cleared from the table. Originally, sweet dishes were interspersed with savory ones and were presented simultaneously at the conclusion of a meal. Even today, cheese can, strictly speaking, be considered part of the dessert course.

A fourteenth-century Parisian menu tells us that the "desserts" included roast bream and darioles, jellies, venison and its traditional accompaniment, frumenty, which was a thick pudding of whole wheat grains and almond milk, sometimes enriched with egg yolks and colored with saffron. The diners had previously enjoyed "blank mang," the barely recognizable forebear of blancmange, which contained shredded chicken blended with whole rice that had been boiled in almond milk, seasoned with sugar and salt and garnished with fried almonds and preserved anise seeds.

In ancient times, people probably ended their meals with fresh or dried fruit, milk or cheese dishes and honey. They are thought to have made sweet foods using maple or birch syrup, wild honey, fruits and seeds — almost a precursor of the modern "health bar." Cave drawings by Australian Aborigines illustrate the harvesting of honeycomb from trees and, many thousands of years later, the first evidence of using honey in cooking comes from the Egyptian tombs of the third millenium BC. Cakes and stewed fruits containing honey were among the foods placed in the pyramids to nourish the occupant on his journey to the next world.

Sugarcane, which probably originated around the Bay of Bengal, was known as a sweetener in India for centuries before it replaced honey about the third century AD. Sugar arrived in Europe with the returning Crusaders around the thirteenth century, but it wasn't until the 1500s that it became commonplace and Italian confectioners achieved notoriety for their spun sugar sculptures.

When Catherine de Medici left Florence in 1533 to marry the future Henri II she took with her a number of Italian pastrycooks and chefs who are credited with introducing a host of culinary novelties to the French court. They include choux pastry and ice cream, of which a different flavor is said to have been prepared for each day of the royal wedding festivities. Iced desserts and drinks had been invented many thousands of years earlier by the Chinese who taught the art to the Arabs, who mixed fruit syrups chilled with snow to make "sharbets," thus providing the basis of today's sorbet and sherbet.

However, it wasn't until the seventeenth

century that ice cream reached the French masses via an establishment called Procope, which now enjoys the reputation of being the oldest café in Paris.

Significant dates in dessert's history include 1638, when almond tartlets were invented by Ragueneau and later immortalized in print in Rostand's *Cyrano de Bergerac*, and 1740, when the baba is believed to have been introduced to France by the Polish king Stanislas Leczcsynski during his exile in Lorraine. Finding the traditional kouglof too dry, he improved it by adding rum and named his creation for his favorite hero Ali Baba. Around 1850 the Julien brothers improved the recipe again, naming it after the gastronome Brillat-Savarin who gave them the secret of making the syrup for soaking the cake. This period also saw the blooming of the pastrycook's art which reached its peak during the eighteenth and nineteenth centuries. This was the era of the reign of Antonin Careme, chef to a host of royal kitchens, architect of amazing sculptural desserts and alleged inventor of nougat, croquembouche, vols-au-vent and meringue, or at least meringue piped into great edifices of calories.

The origin of the first Pavlova is debated between New Zealanders and Australians. According to the Australians, Herbert

Sachse, a former shearer's cook turned Perth hotel chef was asked to prepare a special afternoon tea in 1935. Memories of the recent visit of prima ballerina Pavlova were still fresh in the Australian mind, and Sachse is said to have experimented for a month to create a dessert which was worthy of her name.

The marriage of music and sweet sensations must have been common at the time — Escoffier created peach Melba to honor the great diva, Dame Nellie Melba, when she was appearing in Lohengrin in London. The year was 1892 and the occasion was a dinner hosted by the Duke of Orleans at the Savoy Hotel. To celebrate the guest of honor's triumph she was served a carved ice swan carrying peaches perched on vanilla ice cream topped with spun sugar. On subsequent occasions, perhaps in the interest of expediency, he omitted the swan but added raspberry syrup.

In these busy and health-conscious times desserts have become, paradoxically, both simpler and more sophisticated. As people try to opt for fruit and possibly cheese as healthier after-dinner treats, the special occasion dessert is experiencing a resurgence. With choices ranging from Fanfare and Classic to Folk and Jazz, the recipes in *Dessert — The Grand Finale* will ensure everyone gets their just — delicious — desserts.

The Classics

•

For many, a perfectly orchestrated end to a meal is
a traditional dessert that has withstood the tests of
time and trends and achieved the status of "classic."
These enduring favorites demonstrate why.

INDIVIDUAL GRAND MARNIER SAVARINS WITH BERRIES & WHIPPED CREAM

Serves 8

1 envelope (¼ oz/7g) active dry yeast
2 tablespoons warm water
2 teaspoons sugar
2 tablespoons warm milk
2 eggs
1 cup (3½ oz/100 g)
all-purpose (plain) flour
5 tablespoons (2½ oz/75g) sweet (unsalted)
butter, at room temperature
¼ teaspoon salt
½ cup (4 fl oz/125 ml)
Grand Marnier liqueur
1 teaspoon lemon juice
Whipped cream and berries, for serving
Orange zest (rind), for serving, optional

Whisk together the yeast and warm water in a large bowl. Stir in the sugar and set aside to proof for 10 minutes. Whisk in the milk and eggs. Add the flour and whisk until smooth. Transfer the dough to a clean bowl, cover and set aside until doubled in bulk, about 2 hours. Place the dough in an electric mixer and beat in the butter and salt until thoroughly combined. Transfer the dough to a clean bowl, cover and set aside until doubled in bulk, about 1 hour. Butter 8 individual miniature savarin molds and press equal portions of the dough into each mold. Allow to stand until the dough has doubled in bulk, about 1 hour.
Preheat the oven to 350°F (180°C/Gas 4). Bake the

savarins for 20 minutes, or until light golden brown. Remove from the oven. Brush with a mixture of the Grand Marnier and lemon juice. Allow the savarins to cool for 5 minutes before unmolding and serving with whipped cream and seasonal berries. Decorate with orange zest (rind), if desired.

•

CRÈME BRÛLÉE

Serves 4

1 whole egg
3 egg yolks
⅔ cup (4¾ oz/145 g) sugar
¾ cup (6 fl oz/185 ml) milk
1⅓ cups (10 fl oz/340 ml)
heavy (double) cream
1 teaspoon vanilla extract (essence)
Strawberries, for serving (optional)

Preheat oven to 300°F (150°C/Gas 2). Fill a roasting pan one-third full of water and place in oven. Place the egg and egg yolks and ⅓ cup (2½ oz/75 g) of the sugar in a bowl and whisk together.

Combine the milk and cream in a saucepan and heat to boiling point. Slowly whisk into the egg mixture and then add the vanilla. Cool before straining into four 6-ounce (9 cm diameter) ramekins.

Place in the roasting pan and carefully cover with foil. Bake for 50 minutes. (The custards will not be completely firm.)

Cool and refrigerate until completely cold, preferably overnight.

To serve, preheat broiler (grill). Sprinkle each with 1–2 tablespoons of the remaining sugar and place under broiler, 3–4 inches (6–8 cm) away from the heat. Cook until sugar caramelizes. Remove from the heat and allow the sugar to harden a little before serving.

Serve with strawberries, if desired.

OPPOSITE: Crème Brûlée
PREVIOUS PAGE: Individual Grand Marnier Savarins

SUMMER PUDDINGS
Serves 4

16 slices stale white bread, crusts removed
½ cup (4 oz/125 g) blueberries
½ cup (4 oz/125 g) raspberries
⅓ cup (2¼ oz/65 g) sugar
½ cup (4 oz/125 g) strawberries, chopped
Whipped cream and extra berries,
for serving

STRAWBERRY SAUCE
1 cup (8 oz/250 g) strawberries
3 tablespoons sugar
1 tablespoon water

Line four 6-ounce (9 cm diameter) molds or ramekins with bread, making sure there is no space between the pieces. Cut a "lid" for each from some of the bread.

Place the blueberries and raspberries in a saucepan with the sugar and cook over low heat, gently stirring, for 3–4 minutes. Add the strawberries and cook for 1 minute. Pour the fruit into the prepared molds and place a "lid" over the berries. Cover with plastic wrap and set a weight on top of each pudding. Refrigerate overnight.

Strawberry Sauce: Place the strawberries in a saucepan with the sugar and water and cook over low heat to dissolve the sugar. Bring to a boil and simmer for 3 minutes, or until the strawberries are completely soft. Place in a food processor and process to a purée.

Strain through a fine sieve. Makes 1 cup.

Unmold the puddings and serve with Strawberry Sauce, whipped cream and extra berries.

•

PEACH MELBA
Serves 4

RASPBERRY SAUCE
1 cup (8 oz/250 g) raspberries
2 tablespoons sugar (or to taste)
2 tablespoons boiling water

1 cup (7 oz/220 g) sugar
2½ cups (20 fl oz/600 ml) water
4 firm ripe peaches
Cream or ice cream, for serving

Combine all of the Raspberry Sauce ingredients in a blender or food processor and process to a purée.

Pass the mixture through a sieve to remove the seeds.

Combine the sugar and water in a pan large enough to hold the peaches. Stir over low heat to dissolve sugar; then bring to a boil. Add the whole peaches and simmer for 5–7 minutes. Remove from the syrup and carefully remove the skin.

Serve warm with Raspberry Sauce and cream or ice cream. Any leftover sauce will keep, refrigerated, for 4–5 days.

ABOVE: Peach Melba OPPOSITE: Summer Puddings

PROFITEROLES WITH PASTRY CREAM & TOFFEE ICING

Serves 8

1 cup (8 fl oz/250 ml) water
Pinch of salt
1 tablespoon (½ oz/15 g)
sweet (unsalted) butter
1½ teaspoons sugar
1 cup (4 oz/125 g) all-purpose (plain) flour
4 eggs

PASTRY CREAM
3 egg yolks
¼ cup (2 oz/60 g) sugar
2½ tablespoons all-purpose (plain) flour
1 cup (8 fl oz/250 ml) milk
1 teaspoon vanilla extract (essence)

TOFFEE
1 cup (7 oz/220 g) sugar
2 cups (16 fl oz/500 ml) water

Preheat oven to 375°F (190°C/Gas 5).
Combine the water, salt, butter and sugar in a saucepan. Bring the mixture to a boil. Remove the pan from the heat and stir in the flour, mixing well. Return the saucepan to the heat and cook over medium heat until the dough begins to come away clean from the sides of the pan. Place the dough in an electric mixer and allow to cool slightly before beating in the eggs, one at a time.

Spoon tablespoons of the mixture onto a lightly greased baking sheet. Bake for 25–30 minutes, until golden brown. Turn off the oven. Make a small incision in each profiterole and return to the oven, leaving the door slightly ajar. Leave for 10–15 minutes, allowing the insides to dry out.

Pastry Cream: Put the egg yolks and sugar in a bowl and whisk until pale. Sift in the flour and mix well. Heat the milk to boiling point and gradually whisk into the yolk mixture. Pour this mixture back into the saucepan and stir over low heat for about 7–10 minutes, or until the mixture is thick. Stir in the vanilla. Cool.

Fill each profiterole with pastry cream, using a pastry (piping) bag.

Toffee: Combine the sugar and water in a saucepan and stir over low heat to dissolve the sugar. Bring to a boil and boil, without stirring, for about 5 minutes, or until golden.

Spoon over the filled profiteroles immediately, working quickly, as the toffee will set.

CHOUX PASTRY

1. Bring the combined water, butter and sugar to a boil. Remove from heat and stir in the flour.

3. Cook over medium heat until the dough begins to come away from the sides of the pan.

2. Mix well to thoroughly combine.

4. Place the dough in an electric mixer and allow to cool slightly before beating in the eggs, one at a time.

OPPOSITE: Profiteroles with Pastry Cream & Toffee Icing

MERINGUES FILLED WITH LEMON CURD WITH CREAM & BERRIES

Serves 6–8

9 egg whites
2¼ cups (14¾ oz/460 g) sugar
A little vegetable oil
A little cornstarch (cornflour)
¾ cup (6 fl oz/185 ml) lemon curd
Whipped cream and raspberries,
for serving
Confectioners' (icing) sugar, for serving

Preheat oven to 300°F (140°C/Gas 1).

To make the meringues, beat the egg whites with an electric mixer until stiff but not dry. Gradually add the sugar, beating well after each addition until the mixture is stiff and glossy.

Spoon the egg white mixture into a large pastry (piping) bag fitted with a plain tube (nozzle).

Line 2 baking trays with nonstick paper, lightly oil and then dust with cornstarch (cornflour). Pipe the meringue in 3–4 inch (7–10 cm) circles, making the edges slightly higher than the middle. The mixture should yield about 24 circles.

Bake for 10 minutes, then reduce the oven to 200°F (100°C/Gas ¼) and continue to cook for another 30 minutes, until the meringues are dry.

Turn the oven off, leaving the meringues in the oven for 10 minutes more with the oven door ajar. Remove from the oven and let cool completely before removing from the paper.

Fill one meringue with lemon curd, top with another and fill with whipped cream and top with raspberries or other sweet fruits in season. Dust with confectioners' (icing) sugar, if desired.

Note: The unfilled meringues can be stored in an airtight container for 2 weeks.

RIGHT: Meringues Filled with Lemon Curd

CHRISTMAS PUDDING
Serves 10–12

1 lb (500 g) golden raisins
(sultanas), chopped
1 lb (500 g) dried currants
8 oz (250 g) mixed candied citrus peel
½ cup (4 fl oz/125 ml) brandy
1 lb (500 g) butter
½ cup (4 oz/125 g) packed brown sugar
7 eggs, separated
1 cup (4 oz/125 g)
all-purpose (plain) flour, sifted
Pinch of salt
3 cups (4 oz/125 g) fresh breadcrumbs
¼ teaspoon grated fresh nutmeg
1 tablespoon ground cinnamon
2 teaspoons ground mace or allspice
¼ cup (2 fl oz/60 ml) light (single) cream
Vanilla- or brandy-flavored custard,
for serving

Prepare the fruit and place in a bowl with ¼ cup (2 fl oz/60 ml) of the brandy. Allow to stand, covered, for at least 5 hours.

Cream the butter and brown sugar until light. Add the egg yolks, one at a time, beating well after each addition. Fold in the sifted flour, salt, breadcrumbs and spices alternately with the fruit. Stir in the cream and the remaining ¼ cup (2 fl oz/60 ml) of brandy. Pour into a large heat-proof pudding mold. Cover with 2 rounds each of waxed (greaseproof) paper and then with aluminum foil. Tie the mold securely with string, by wrapping the string around the top of the mold and making a "handle" by tying more string across the top, tying each end onto the string wrapped around the top of the mold.

Put enough water in a saucepan large enough to hold the pudding mold, to come three-fourths of the way up the side of the mold and bring to a boil. Lower the mold into boiling water and boil for 6 hours, continually adding boiling water to the pan to keep the water about three-fourths of the way up the mold. Remove the pudding and set aside for at least a week before serving.

Serve with vanilla- or brandy-flavored custard.

•

CHOCOLATE MOUSSE
Serves 6

1½ lb (750 g) semisweet or bittersweet
(dark) chocolate
½ cup (4 fl oz/125 ml) brewed coffee
½ cup (4 fl oz/125 ml) Scotch whisky
4 egg yolks
1 cup (8 fl oz/250 ml)
heavy (double) cream
¼ cup (1¾ oz/50 g) sugar
8 egg whites
Pinch of salt
Strawberries and whipped cream,
for serving (optional)

Melt the chocolate in the top of a double boiler or *bain marie* over low heat, or in the microwave on low power. Stir in the coffee and whisky. Cool to room temperature. Beat in the egg yolks, one at a time. Whip the cream until thick, gradually adding the sugar until stiff peaks form.

Beat the egg whites with a pinch of salt until stiff. Fold the egg whites into the cream. Fold this mixture into the chocolate mixture. Pour into 6 individual serving glasses and refrigerate for 2 hours before serving.

ABOVE: Chocolate Mousse OPPOSITE: Christmas Pudding

WINE FRUIT GELATIN (JELLY)
Serves 8

4 apricots, halved and pitted
6 plums, halved and pitted
⅔ cup (5 oz/155 g) seedless green grapes
1 cup (8 oz/250 g) cherries
1 cup (8 oz/250 g) other fruit
(but not pineapple, pawpaw or kiwi as
these contain an acid that prevents the
gelatin setting)
2 oz (60 g) unflavored gelatin
½ cup (4 fl oz/125 ml) boiling water
2 cups (16 fl oz/500 ml) sweet white wine
2⅓ cups (18½ fl oz/585 ml)
clear apple juice
Whipped cream or ice cream, for serving

Prepare the fruit. Combine the gelatin and boiling water and stir until the gelatin is completely dissolved. Add the wine and apple juice and mix to combine. Pour one-third of the wine mixture into a lightly oiled 8-cup (2 liter) glass dish or mold and top with one-fourth of the fruit. Place in refrigerator for at least 30 minutes, or until set. Repeat with remaining liquid and fruit and leave to set for at least 1 hour and 30 minutes.

When all set, unmold and serve with whipped cream or ice cream.

ABOVE: Crèmes Caramel OPPOSITE: Wine Fruit Gelatin

CRÈMES CARAMEL
Serves 4

1 whole egg
3 egg yolks
½ cup (3½ oz/100 g) sugar
Pinch of salt
½ cup (4 fl oz/125 ml) milk
1½ cups (12 fl oz/375 ml)
heavy (double) cream

CARAMEL
½ cup (3½ oz/100 g) sugar
3 tablespoons water

CANDIED ORANGE ZEST
2 oranges
½ cup (4 fl oz/125 ml) water
½ cup (3½ oz/100 g) sugar

Preheat oven to 300°F (150°C/Gas 2). Place a roasting pan one-third full of water in the oven. Lightly grease four 6-ounce (9 cm diameter) ramekins with oil. Whisk together the egg, egg yolks, sugar and salt. Heat the milk and cream to boiling point. Whisk into the egg mixture. Cool completely.

Caramel: Combine the sugar and 2 tablespoons of the water in a saucepan. Stir over low heat until the sugar dissolves. Bring to a boil and boil, without stirring, for about 5 minutes, until golden. Remove from the heat and stir in the remaining water. Working quickly, divide the caramel among the ramekins, tilting each to coat the bottom. Set aside to cool.

Pour the custard into the ramekins and place in the baking dish. Carefully cover with aluminum foil and cook for 50 minutes. They should be firm at the edges and a little shaky in the middle. Cool and refrigerate, preferably overnight. Unmold.

Candied Orange Zest: Remove the zest (rind) from the oranges and cut into julienne. Blanch for 30 seconds in boiling water. Heat the water with the sugar over low heat to dissolve the sugar. Bring to a boil and cook for a further minute. Add the zest and cook for 1 minute. Remove with a slotted spoon. Serve the Crèmes Caramel with the Candied Orange Zest.

National Anthems

·

Raise the flag in a salute to this worldly selection of favorites,
whether American, Swiss, Australian, Mexican, Canadian
or Italian. Sing the praises of these international
treats — a global chorus of glorious desserts.

BLACK FOREST CAKE

Serves 10–12

8 tablespoons (4 oz/125 g)
sweet (unsalted) butter,
at room temperature
¾ cup (5 oz/155 g) sugar
2 eggs
6½ oz (200 g) semisweet (dark) chocolate,
melted and cooled
2 cups (7 oz/220 g) self-rising flour
2 tablespoons unsweetened cocoa powder
1 teaspoon baking powder
1 cup (8 fl oz/250 ml) milk
1¾ oz (50 g) semisweet (dark) chocolate,
coarsely chopped

FILLING
¼ cup (2 fl oz/60 ml) kirsch
¼ cup (2 fl oz/60 ml) cherry jelly or jam
3 cups (24 fl oz/750 ml), heavy (double)
cream, whipped
1 (12–15 oz/375–470 g) jar pitted sour
(black) cherries, drained
5 oz (155 g) semisweet (dark)
chocolate, melted

Preheat oven to 350°F (180°C/Gas 4). Butter a 10-inch (25 cm) round cake pan and line with parchment or waxed (greaseproof) paper.

Beat the butter and sugar until creamy. Add the eggs, one at a time, beating well after each addition. Stir in the chocolate. Sift together the flour, cocoa and baking powder and fold into the butter mixture alternately with the milk and chopped chocolate. Pour the batter into the prepared pan and bake for 55–60 minutes, until a skewer inserted in the middle comes out clean. Remove from the oven and turn out onto a wire rack to cool. When cool, cut the cake horizontally into 3 layers.

Filling: Brush one side of each layer with a little of the kirsch. Spread the bottom layer with half of the jelly or jam, some of the whipped cream, and one-third of the cherries. Top with the second layer and repeat with the remaining jelly, some of the cream and one-third of the cherries. Top with the remaining layer and spread the sides and top of the cake with the remaining cream. Decorate with the remaining cherries and drizzle with the melted chocolate. Refrigerate until ready to serve.

•

SPOTTED DICK

Serves 4

½ cup (4 fl oz/125 ml) brandy
¾ cup (6 oz/185 g) currants
5 tablespoons (2¾ oz/80 g) sweet
(unsalted) butter
½ cup (4 oz/125 g) sugar
3 eggs
1⅔ cups (6 oz/185 g) self-rising flour
1 teaspoon baking powder
2 tablespoons light corn syrup or golden
syrup, plus ¼ cup (2 fl oz/60 ml), for serving
Light (single) cream, for serving

Heat the brandy until it is just warm to the touch. Place the currants in a bowl and pour in the warmed brandy. Set aside for at least 3 hours.

Preheat oven to 350°F (180°C/Gas 4). Butter four 1-cup (8 fl oz/250 ml) pudding molds, custard cups or ramekins. Fill a baking dish (large enough to hold the molds) half-full with water. Place in oven. Cream the butter and sugar until light and fluffy. Add the eggs, one at a time, beating well after each addition. Add the sifted flour and baking powder and beat. Add the currants and brandy and stir. Pour the batter into the molds, filling them three-fourths full. Cover loosely with aluminum foil and place in the baking dish. Cook for 45–50 minutes, or until a skewer inserted in the middle of a pudding comes out clean and they are puffed and golden.

Place the extra syrup in a small saucepan and cook over low heat for 3–4 minutes, until warm.

Serve the Spotted Dick warm with cream and the warmed syrup.

PREVIOUS PAGE: Black Forest Cake (Germany)

OPPOSITE: Spotted Dick (England)

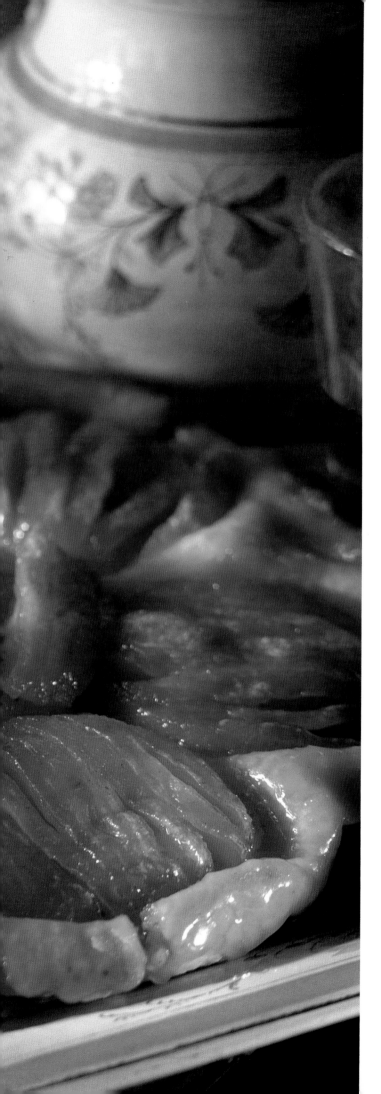

TARTE TATIN
Serves 4

PASTRY
2 cups (8 oz/250 g)
all-purpose (plain) flour
2 teaspoons sugar
7 tablespoons (3½ oz/100 g)
sweet (unsalted) butter
1 egg yolk
3 tablespoons ice water

APPLES
3 green apples, such as Granny Smiths
6 tablespoons (3 oz/90 g)
sweet (unsalted) butter
1 cup (6½ oz/200 g) sugar

Pastry: Combine the flour, sugar and butter in a food processor and process to a coarse meal. Add the egg yolk and, with the motor running, enough ice water so that the dough just forms a mass. Do not overprocess. Wrap the pastry in plastic wrap and refrigerate for 30 minutes.

Apples: Peel and core the apples. Cut in half and slice thinly.

Melt the butter in an 8-inch (22 cm) nonstick frying pan that has a metal or ovenproof handle. Sprinkle the sugar evenly on the bottom of the pan. Remove from the heat and arrange the apple slices closely together and slightly overlapping in concentric circles on top of the butter/sugar mixture. Cook the apples over moderate heat for 15–20 minutes, until a deep golden, bubbly caramel has formed. Remove the pan from the heat and allow to cool slightly, at least 5 minutes.

Preheat oven to 425°F (220°C/Gas 7).

Roll out the pastry to a circle slightly larger than the pan, about 10 inches (25 cm) and ½–¾ inch (1½– 2 cm) thick. Gently set the pastry over the apples to completely cover, tucking the pastry in at the edges. Work quickly as the dough will soften. Bake for 20– 25 minutes, until the pastry is crisp and golden.

LEFT: Tarte Tatin (France)

Let the tart cool in the pan for about 10 minutes. Invert onto a serving platter. If any apple sticks to the bottom of the pan, transfer it to the top of the tart. Serve warm with thick cream or crème fraîche.

•

LAMINGTONS
Makes 6

4 eggs
¾ cup (5 oz/155 g) sugar
1 cup (4 oz/125 g) all-purpose (plain) flour
4 tablespoons (2 oz/60 g)
butter, melted and cooled
8 oz (250 g) semisweet
(dark) chocolate
1 tablespoon orange-flavored liqueur
1 cup (3½ oz/100 g) sweetened
(desiccated) shredded coconut
Heavy (double) cream, for serving

Preheat oven to 350°F (180°C/Gas 4). Butter an 8-inch (20 cm) square cake pan. Line the bottom with parchment or waxed (greaseproof) paper.
Combine the eggs and sugar in a large bowl and beat until the mixture is thick and creamy, 5–7 minutes. Sift in half of the flour and gently fold in. Fold in the remaining flour. Carefully and quickly fold in the butter. Pour into the prepared pan and

ABOVE: Lamingtons (Australia)
OPPOSITE: Chocolate & Almond Strudel (Switzerland)

bake for 20 minutes, until the cake feels springy to the touch. Turn out onto a wire rack to cool completely.
Melt the chocolate and orange liqueur (if desired) together in a double boiler over hot, not simmering, water.
Sprinkle the coconut over a large plate or tray. Cut the cooled cake into 6 equal pieces. Holding a piece of cake with a fork, dip into the chocolate, swirling so that all of the cake is covered. Roll in coconut and set aside. Repeat with the remaining cake pieces.
Serve immediately with cream.
Lamingtons can be stored in an airtight container for up to 2 days.

•

CHOCOLATE & ALMOND STRUDEL
Serves 6

1½ cups (9 oz/280 g) ground almonds
3 eggs
1 teaspoon almond extract (essence)
½ cup (3½ oz/100 g) sugar
¾ cup (2½ oz/75 g)
sliced (flaked) almonds
6 sheets filo pastry
3 tablespoons (1½ oz/45 g) butter,
6½ oz (200 g) semisweet (dark)
chocolate, grated

CHOCOLATE SAUCE
(Makes 1½ cups/12 fl oz/375 ml)
1 cup (8 fl oz/250 ml) heavy (double) cream
6½ oz (200 g) semisweet (dark) chocolate,
broken into pieces

Preheat oven to 350°F (180°C/Gas 4). Line a baking sheet with aluminum foil and butter the foil. Combine the ground almonds, eggs, almond extract (essence) and sugar in a food processor. Process to combine. Add the sliced (flaked) almonds and pulse until the sliced almonds are just combined.

Place 1 sheet of filo pastry on the baking sheet with a long side in front of you. Brush with melted butter and top with a second sheet. Brush this with melted butter and repeat with a third sheet. Sprinkle one-fourth of the grated chocolate on top. Add the fourth, fifth and sixth sheets, brushing each with melted butter. Sprinkle the top piece of filo with half of the remaining chocolate. Spread the almond filling on top of the bottom third of the filo pastry layers, then sprinkle on the remaining chocolate. Roll up as you would a jelly (Swiss) roll. Brush the top of the roll with melted butter and place in the middle of the baking sheet. Bake for 25–30 minutes, or until the pastry is crisp and golden.

Chocolate Sauce: Bring the cream to a boil in a medium saucepan. Remove from the heat and stir in the chocolate. Let stand for 10 minutes before stirring until smooth.

Slice the Strudel and serve drizzled with the Chocolate Sauce.

●

MEXICAN FLAN
Serves 6

2 cups (7 oz/220 g) sugar
¾ cup (6 fl oz/185 ml) water
6 eggs
1 teaspoon vanilla extract (essence)
1¼ cups (10 fl oz/315 ml) milk
1½ cups (12 fl oz/375 ml)
heavy (double) cream
½ cup (1¾ oz/50 g) blanched almonds,
toasted, for serving
Cream, for serving

Preheat oven to 350°F (180°C/Gas 4).

Combine three-fourths of the sugar and all of the water in a saucepan. Stir over low heat to dissolve the sugar. Bring to a boil and boil until golden, about 5 minutes. Pour the caramel into an 8-inch

OPPOSITE: Mexican Flan (Mexico) (top)
and Tiramisu (Italy) (bottom)

(20 cm) round cake pan and swirl to completely cover the base.

Beat together the eggs and the remaining sugar until pale. Beat in the vanilla. Combine the milk and cream in a saucepan and heat to boiling point. Strain into the egg mixture, whisking constantly. Pour the mixture over the caramel and place in the oven. Bake for 35 minutes, or until the custard is set. (Check by gently shaking the cake pan; when the custard is only just wobbly, it has set.) Remove from the oven and let cool to room temperature. Cover with plastic wrap and refrigerate overnight.

To serve, remove plastic, run a knife around the edge of the custard and invert onto a serving plate. Decorate with the toasted almonds and serve with cream.

●

TIRAMISU
Serves 4

3 eggs, separated
2 tablespoons sugar
8 oz (250 g) mascarpone cheese,
at room temperature
2 tablespoons dark rum
12 ladyfingers (sponge fingers)
⅓ cup (2½ fl oz/75 ml)
brewed strong black coffee
¼ cup (¾ oz/20 g)
unsweetened cocoa powder

Whisk together the egg yolks and sugar until thick and pale. Fold in the mascarpone and rum. Beat the egg whites until stiff peaks form. Fold the whites into the mascarpone mixture.

Brush each ladyfinger (sponge finger) all over with some of the coffee. Line the base of a 6–8 cup, 3-inch (8 cm) deep, serving dish with a single layer of ladyfingers. Spread half of the mascarpone mixture on top and dust with half of the cocoa powder. Add another layer of ladyfingers and repeat, finishing with a mascarpone layer. Refrigerate overnight.

Dust the remaining cocoa powder on the top just before serving.

LATTICE APPLE PIE
Serves 8–10

SWEET SHORTCRUST PASTRY
2 cups (8 oz/250 g) all-purpose (plain) flour
⅓ cup (1¾ oz/50 g) confectioners'
(icing) sugar
½ cup (5½ oz/170 g) sweet (unsalted)
butter, cut into small pieces
1 egg yolk
⅙ cup (1½ fl oz/45 ml) cold water

FILLING
5½ lb (2¾ kg) Granny Smith apples
1 cup (7 oz/220 g) sugar
⅓ cup (3½ oz/100 g) sweet (unsalted) butter
Grated zest (rind) of ½ lemon
1 egg white, lightly beaten

Pastry: Sift together the flour and confectioners' (icing) sugar. Make a well in the center and add the butter. Mix with fingertips until the mixture resembles coarse breadcrumbs.

Mix in the egg yolks and cold water, working quickly to form a mass. Push the mixture with the heel of your hand to thoroughly combine. Roll into a ball, cover with plastic wrap and refrigerate for 1 hour.

Preheat oven to 350°F (180°C/Gas 4).

Roll out the pastry to line a deep 10-inch (25 cm) pie plate, reserving and slicing some of the pastry for the lattice. Cover with parchment or waxed (greaseproof) paper and baking weights (dried beans or rice). Bake for 15 minutes.

Filling: Peel and core the apples and cut into thin slices. Combine the apples, sugar, butter and lemon zest (rind) in a large saucepan. Cook over low heat until the apples soften, about 10 minutes.

Brush the partially cooked sweet shortcrust pastry shell with egg white and fill with the apple mixture. Top the pie with a lattice pattern, using the reserved pastry, and brush with a little egg white. Bake for 30–35 minutes.

*RIGHT: Pumpkin Pie (America) (top)
and Lattice Apple Pie (America) (bottom)*

PUMPKIN PIE
Serves 8–10

PRALINE PECANS
½ cup (3½ oz/100 g) sugar
¼ cup (2 fl oz/60 ml) water
2 cups (6½ oz/200 g) whole pecans, roasted

FILLING
6 eggs
1 cup (7 oz/220 g) packed brown sugar
1 cup (8 fl oz/250 ml) light corn syrup or
golden syrup
3 cups (24 fl oz/750 ml) heavy (double) cream
3 cups cooked, mashed pumpkin
(approx. 3 lb/1.5 kg raw)
1 tablespoon dark rum
1 teaspoon freshly grated nutmeg
¼ teaspoon salt
1 prepared sweet shortcrust pastry shell
(see Lattice Apple Pie recipe)

Praline Pecans: Insert a toothpick into each of the pecans. Set aside.

Combine the sugar and water in a saucepan and stir over low heat to dissolve the sugar. Bring to a boil and boil until golden, about 5–7 minutes. Using the toothpick, quickly dip each pecan into the toffee. Place pecans on an oiled wire rack to set, about 2 minutes.

Preheat oven to 350°F (180°C/Gas 4).

Filling: Whisk together the eggs and brown sugar in a bowl. Add the syrup and mix until smooth. Stir in the cream, pumpkin purée, rum, nutmeg and salt. Combine thoroughly. Pour into the prepared pastry shell; bake for 35–40 minutes, until firm to the touch in the middle. Let cool before decorating with the Praline Pecans.

•

MAPLE TART
Serves 8–10

PASTRY
2 cups (8 oz/250 g) all-purpose (plain) flour
11 tablespoons (5½ oz/170 g) sweet
(unsalted) butter
2 tablespoons sugar
1 whole egg
1–2 tablespoons ice water
1 egg white, beaten, for pastry cut-outs

SWEET SHORTCRUST PASTRY SHELL

1. Sift together the flour and confectioners' (icing) sugar onto a work surface or into a large mixing bowl. Make a well in the center and add the butter, cut into small pieces. Mix until mixture resembles coarse breadcrumbs.

2. Mix in the egg yolks and the cold water, working quickly to form a mass. Push the mixture with the heel of your hand to thoroughly combine, then re-form into a ball. Refrigerate for 1 hour before using.

3. Roll out pastry to line a pie plate or pan and cover with parchment or waxed (greaseproof) paper. Scatter with baking weights, dried beans or rice, and bake for 15 minutes, or until a pale golden color.

ABOVE: Maple Tart (Canada)

FILLING
5 eggs, beaten
1 cup (7 oz/220 g) packed brown sugar
¾ cup (6 fl oz/185 ml) maple syrup
5½ tablespoons (2¾ oz/80 g) sweet
(unsalted) butter, melted

Preheat oven to 350°F (180°C/Gas 4).

Pastry: Place the flour, butter and sugar in a food processor and process to a coarse meal. Add the egg and 1 tablespoon of the water and pulse until the mixture comes together. (It may be necessary to add more water, a little at a time.) Remove and wrap in plastic wrap. Refrigerate for 30 minutes. Roll out the pastry to line a 1-inch (2.5 cm) deep, 11-inch (28 cm) tart pan with a removable base. Line the pastry shell with parchment or waxed (greaseproof) paper and fill with baking weights, dried beans or rice. Bake the pastry shell for 15 minutes. Remove the weights and allow to cool.

Using a small sharp knife or cookie cutter, cut out maple leaf shapes from any remaining pastry. Line a baking sheet with parchment or waxed (greaseproof) paper. Brush the pastry shapes with a little of the beaten egg white, place on the prepared baking sheet and bake for 15 minutes, until golden.

Filling: Combine the eggs, brown sugar, maple syrup and melted butter in a bowl. Mix until combined. Brush the cooled pastry shell with a little of the beaten egg white and pour in the filling. Bake the tart for 40–45 minutes, until filling just wobbles when shaken. Allow to cool.

Decorate the tart with the maple leaf pastry shapes and serve.

All that Jazz

•

Take after-dinner delights from the mainstream to the legendary with a bit of tasteful pizazz. They'll bop and swing to the sweet, subtle tones of these delectable desserts!

CHOCOLATE ORANGE TRUFFLE CAKES

Serves 6

TOFFEED ORANGE ZEST
1 cup (8 fl oz/250 ml) water
1 cup (6½ oz/200 g) sugar
Zest (rind) of 1 orange, cut into julienne

TRUFFLE CAKE
8 tablespoons (4 oz/125 g) sweet (unsalted)
butter, at room temperature
¾ cup (5 oz/155 g) sugar
2 eggs
6½ oz (200 g) semisweet (dark)
chocolate, melted and cooled
1 tablespoon Cointreau or
other orange liqueur
1 tablespoon grated orange zest (rind)
2 cups (7 oz/220 g) self-rising flour
2 tablespoons unsweetened cocoa powder
1 teaspoon baking powder
1 cup (8 fl oz/250 ml) milk

DOUBLE GANACHE ICING
8 oz (250 g) semisweet (dark) chocolate,
coarsely chopped
1½ cups (12 fl oz/375 ml)
heavy (double) cream

Toffeed Orange Zest: Combine the water with the sugar in a saucepan and stir over low heat to dissolve the sugar. Bring the syrup to a boil and boil until golden. Remove from the heat and, working quickly, dip each piece of zest (rind) into the toffee syrup using tongs. Place the zest on a lightly oiled wire rack to harden.

Truffle Cake: Preheat oven to 400°F (200°C/Gas 6). Beat the butter and sugar until creamy. Add the eggs, one at a time, beating well after each addition. Stir in the chocolate, Cointreau and grated orange zest. Sift together the flour, cocoa and baking powder and fold into the chocolate mixture, alternately with the milk. Divide the batter among 6 nonstick muffin cups. Bake for 40 minutes, or until a skewer inserted in the middle of one muffin comes out clean. Turn out onto a wire rack to cool.

Double Ganache Icing: Place the chocolate in a metal bowl. Put the cream into a saucepan and bring just to a boil. Pour the cream over the chocolate. Let stand for 2–3 minutes and then stir until smooth. Set aside half of the mixture in a warm place and refrigerate the remainder until cold but not solid, about 20 minutes.

Beat the cooled ganache mixture with an electric beater until spreadable. Spread over the tops of the cooled cakes and chill until firm, about 10–15 minutes. When firm, pour over the remaining chocolate cream mixture. Allow to set, about 5 minutes. Decorate with Toffeed Orange Zest and serve.

●

UPSIDE-DOWN GINGERBREAD WITH PEARS

Serves 8

1 cinnamon stick
½ cup (3½ oz/100 g) sugar
1 tablespoon fresh lemon juice
2 cups (16 fl oz/500 ml) water
3 pears
8 tablespoons (4 oz/125 g) sweet
(unsalted) butter
1 cup (7 oz/220 g) packed brown sugar
1 cup (4 oz/125 g) all-purpose (plain) flour
½ teaspoon baking soda
(bicarbonate of soda)
1 teaspoon ground cinnamon
¼ teaspoon grated nutmeg
1 egg, beaten
½ cup (4 fl oz/125 ml) light corn syrup or
golden syrup
4 tablespoons (2 oz/60g) sweet
(unsalted) butter, melted
Crème fraîche, for serving

OPPOSITE: Upside-down Gingerbread with Pears
PREVIOUS PAGE: Chocolate Orange Truffle Cakes

Preheat oven to 350°F (180°C/Gas 4).

Grease a 10-inch (25 cm) cake pan.

Place the cinnamon stick, sugar, lemon juice and water in a large saucepan and stir over low heat to dissolve the sugar. Bring to a boil. Meanwhile, peel, core, and halve the pears. Add them to the saucepan and poach for 5 minutes. Remove the pears from the syrup and allow to cool.

Place the butter and brown sugar in a saucepan and bring to a boil, stirring until combined. Pour the mixture into the prepared pan. Arrange the pears, cut-sides up, on top.

Sift the flour, baking soda (bicarbonate of soda), cinnamon and nutmeg into a large bowl.

Combine the egg, light corn or golden syrup and butter, whisking well, and stir into the dry ingredients. Beat the mixture well with an electric mixer. Pour over the pears.

Bake for 1 hour, until a skewer inserted in the middle comes out barely moist.

Allow to stand on a wire rack for at least 30 minutes. Turn out onto a serving platter. Serve warm, with crème fraîche.

NUT TART
Serves 8–10

PASTRY

2 cups (8 oz/250 g) all-purpose (plain) flour

11 tablespoons (5½ oz/170 g) cold, sweet (unsalted) butter

2 tablespoons granulated sugar

1 whole egg

1–2 tablespoons cold water

1 egg white, beaten

FILLING

6 eggs, beaten

1 cup (7 oz/220 g) packed brown sugar

¾ cup (6 fl oz/185 ml) light corn syrup or golden syrup

4½ tablespoons (2¾ oz/80 g) sweet (unsalted) butter, melted

½ cup (2 oz/60 g) hazelnuts

½ cup (3 oz/90 g) macadamia nuts

½ cup (1¾ oz/50 g) pecan halves

½ cup (1¾ oz/50 g) walnut halves

ABOVE: Nut Tart

Preheat oven to 350°F (180°C/Gas 4).

Pastry: Place the flour, butter and sugar in a food processor and process to a coarse meal. Add the egg and 1 tablespoon of the water and pulse until the mixture comes together. It may be necessary to add more water, a little at a time, until the mixture comes together. Remove and wrap in plastic wrap. Refrigerate for 30 minutes.

Roll out the pastry and line a 9-inch, 2-inch deep (22 cm, 5 cm deep) tart pan. Cover with parchment or waxed (greaseproof) paper and sprinkle with baking weights, dried beans or rice. Bake for 15 minutes.

Filling: Combine the eggs, brown sugar, syrup and melted butter in a bowl. Mix until combined and then stir in the nuts.

Remove the pastry from the oven and remove the weights and paper. Brush the pastry with beaten egg white and pour the filling into the tart shell. Return to the oven and bake for 40–45 minutes, until the filling just wobbles when shaken. Remove from the oven and allow to cool before serving.

THREE-LAYERED CHOCOLATE TERRINE
Serves 10–12

7 oz (220 g) semisweet (dark) chocolate
6½ oz (200 g) milk chocolate
5 oz (155 g) white chocolate
3 cups (24 fl oz/750 ml)
heavy (double) cream

Chop the chocolate into small pieces and place in three separate bowls.

Heat the cream to boiling point and pour 1¼ cups (10 fl oz/315 ml) over the semisweet (dark) chocolate, 1 cup (8 fl oz/250 ml) over the milk chocolate, and ¾ cup (6 fl oz/185 ml) over the white chocolate. Whisk each chocolate until smooth.

Cover each bowl with plastic wrap and cool to room temperature. Refrigerate until thick, but not hardened, about 2½ hours. Line a 9-inch (22 cm) round springform pan with plastic wrap or foil, leaving a 1-inch (2.5 cm) overhang around the top of the pan.

ABOVE: Three-layered Chocolate Terrine

Remove the semisweet chocolate mixture from the fridge and beat, using an electric mixer, until thick, soft peaks form. Pour into the prepared pan, cover with plastic wrap and freeze for 5 minutes. Remove the plastic wrap; repeat with the other chocolates. Cover the pan with plastic wrap and freeze overnight. Remove the terrine from the freezer 15 minutes before serving. Just before serving, remove the sides of the pan, peel off the foil or plastic wrap and slice into wedges to serve.

•

PAVLOVA WITH CHOCOLATE HAZELNUT CREAM
Serves 8

MERINGUE
8 egg whites,
at room temperature
1½ cups (10 oz/315 g) sugar

CHOCOLATE HAZELNUT CREAM
1¼ cups (10 fl oz/315 ml)
heavy (double) cream, whipped
1 cup (3½ oz/100 g) ground hazelnuts
4 oz (125 g) semisweet (dark) chocolate,
melted and cooled
¼ cup (1 oz/30 g) chopped hazelnuts

Meringue: Preheat oven to 250°F (130°C/Gas ½). Line a baking sheet with parchment or waxed (greaseproof) paper.
In a large bowl beat the egg whites until stiff but not dry. Add ½ cup (3½ oz/100 g) of the sugar and beat until it completely dissolves. Continue beating and adding the remaining sugar until combined.
Using a spatula, shape the meringue into two 8-inch (20 cm) rounds on the prepared baking sheet. Make a dip in the center of one (for the bottom layer) and a peak in the center of the other (for the top layer).
Bake the meringues for 10 minutes. Reduce the heat

RIGHT: Pavlova with Chocolate Hazelnut Cream

to 225°F (110°C/Gas ¼) and bake for another 45–50 minutes, until meringues are dry and sound hollow when gently tapped.

Remove from the oven and allow meringues to cool on a wire rack.

Chocolate Hazelnut Cream: Fold together the whipped cream, ground hazelnuts and half of the melted chocolate. Spread the bottom round of the meringue with the cream mixture and top with the remaining meringue round. Drizzle with the remaining chocolate and sprinkle with chopped hazelnuts.

•

POACHED TAMARILLOS
Serves 4

12–16 tamarillos
2¼ cups (8 oz/250 g) sugar
3 cups (24 fl oz/750 ml) water
Light (single) cream, for serving

Plunge the tamarillos into boiling water for 5 seconds. Transfer to a bowl of ice water and peel off the skins, leaving the stems intact.

Combine the sugar and water in a saucepan and stir over low heat until the sugar dissolves. Bring to a boil. Reduce the heat, add the tamarillos and poach for 10 minutes. (It may be necessary to work in batches of 6.)

Remove the tamarillos and slice almost in half, leaving the stem end intact. Return all of the tamarillos to the poaching liquid and let stand for 20 minutes, until they turn a rich red color. Serve, drizzled with cream.

ABOVE: Tropical Fruit Salad with Piña Colada Dressing
OPPOSITE: Poached Tamarillos

TROPICAL FRUIT SALAD WITH PIÑA COLADA DRESSING
Serves 6–8

FRUIT SALAD
1 cantaloupe (rockmelon)
2 papayas (pawpaws)
10 oz (315 g) fresh lychees
4 kiwi fruits

DRESSING
1 lb (500 g) pineapple flesh
⅓ cup (2½ fl oz/75 ml) coconut milk
2 tablespoons white rum

Fruit Salad: Peel and slice all of the fruit into bite-size pieces and toss together in a serving bowl.

Dressing: Place the pineapple in a food processor and process to a purée. Strain through a sieve. Return to the processor, add the coconut milk and rum and process until combined. Pour the dressing over the fruit salad and serve.

APRICOT CREAM CHEESE CHOCOLATE BROWNIES

Serves 4

¾ cup (3 oz/90 g) dried apricots, chopped
3 tablespoons brandy
5 oz (155 g) cream cheese
2 tablespoons (1 oz/30 g) sweet
(unsalted) butter
¼ cup (1¾ oz/50 g) sugar
1 egg

3½ tablespoons (1¾ oz/50 g) sweet
(unsalted) butter
4 oz (125 g) semisweet (dark) chocolate,
chopped
2 eggs
¾ cup (5 oz/155 g) sugar
1 teaspoon vanilla extract (essence)
½ cup (2 oz/60 g) all-purpose (plain) flour
½ teaspoon baking powder
¼ teaspoon salt
½ cup (2 oz/60 g) chopped walnuts
Whipped cream or ice cream, for serving

Place the dried apricots in a bowl and pour over the brandy. Allow to stand for at least 1 hour.

Beat the cream cheese and butter until smooth, gradually add the sugar and continue beating until creamy. Add the egg and beat to combine. Stir in the apricots and brandy.

Preheat oven to 350°F (180°C/Gas 4). Grease an 8-inch (20 cm) square cake pan.

Heat the butter over low heat. When half-melted, add the chocolate and stir to combine. When the chocolate is melted, remove from heat and set aside. Beat the eggs until light and foamy, gradually add the sugar and beat until pale and thickened. Fold in the chocolate and butter mixture, the vanilla and sifted dry ingredients. Pour two-thirds of the chocolate mixture into the prepared pan. Pour the Apricot Cream Cheese on top. Spoon on the remaining chocolate mixture. Using a skewer, swirl the Apricot Cream Cheese through the chocolate mixture. Bake until a skewer inserted into the middle of the cake comes out barely moist, about 35–40 minutes. Cool completely in the pan before turning out and slicing to serve.

Serve with whipped cream or ice cream.

OPPOSITE: Apricot Cream Cheese Chocolate Brownies

APRICOT CREAM CHEESE CHOCOLATE BROWNIES

1. Stir the apricots and brandy into the cream cheese, butter, sugar and egg mixture.

3. Pour the apricot cream cheese on top and add the remaining chocolate mixture in spoonfuls.

2. Stir the chocolate mixture well to combine and then pour two-thirds into the prepared pan.

4. Using a skewer, swirl the Apricot Cream Cheese through the chocolate mixture.

MISSISSIPPI MUD CAKE

Makes one 9-inch (22 cm) round cake

16 tablespoons (8 oz/250 g)
sweet (unsalted) butter
1 tablespoon whiskey
¾ cup (6 oz/185 g) sugar
8 oz (250 g) semisweet (dark)
chocolate, chopped
1½ cups (12 fl oz/375 ml) hot water
1½ cups (6 oz/185 g)
self-rising flour
¼ cup (1 oz/30 g) cocoa powder
2 eggs
1 teaspoon vanilla extract (essence)
Heavy (double) cream, for serving
1 sprig mint, for decoration (optional)

Preheat oven to 350°F (180°C/Gas 4).

Melt the butter in a saucepan. Add the whiskey, sugar, chocolate and water. Stir over low heat until the chocolate is just melted and the mixture is smooth. Sift the flour and cocoa powder together and gradually beat into the chocolate mixture. Add the eggs and vanilla and beat until combined.

Pour the mixture into a greased and lined 9-inch (22 cm) round cake pan and bake for 40–45 minutes, until a skewer inserted in the center comes out clean. Leave the cake in the pan for 15 minutes before turning out to cool.

Serve warm or cold with cream and decorated with a sprig of mint, if desired.

RIGHT: Mississippi Mud Cake

Duets

•

Create a sensuous atmosphere of romance — softly lit table, tender music and a deliciously tempting dessert that invites indulgence. These seductive desserts are a perfect serenade for the apple of your eye.

PECAN TARTLETS
Serves 2

PASTRY
2½ cups (8 oz/250 g)
all-purpose (plain) flour
2 teaspoons sugar
10 tablespoons (5 oz/155 g)
cold sweet (unsalted) butter
1 egg yolk
1–2 tablespoons water

FILLING
2 eggs
½ cup (3½ oz/100 g) packed brown sugar
¼ cup (2 fl oz/60 ml)
light corn syrup or golden syrup
2½ tablespoons (1¼ oz/40 g)
sweet (unsalted) butter, melted
½ cup (2 oz/60 g) chopped pecans
½ cup (2 oz/60 g) pecan halves
Crème fraîche, for serving

Preheat oven to 325°F (170°C/Gas 3).
Pastry: Place the flour, sugar and butter in a food processor. Process to coarse crumbs. Add the egg yolk and 1 tablespoon of the ice water and pulse until dough comes together — if necessary add a little more water.

Roll out the pastry to a thickness of ½ inch (1 cm). Line two 4-inch (10 cm) tartlet pans that have removable bases with the pastry. (Any leftover pastry can be kept, frozen, for up to 1 month.)

Line the pastry shells with parchment or waxed (greaseproof) paper and fill with baking weights (dried beans or rice).

Bake for 10 minutes.

Remove from the oven. Remove the weights and paper and set aside.

Filling: Beat the eggs. Stir in the brown sugar and light corn or golden syrup. Stir in the butter and chopped pecans and combine thoroughly. Pour the mixture into the pastry shells. Arrange the pecan halves in a pattern on top.

Bake the tartlets for 20–25 minutes, until the pastry is lightly browned and the middle of the tartlets are set. Remove from the oven and allow to cool a little before unmolding and serving with crème fraîche.

•

BERRIES IN WHIPPED CREAM WITH ALMOND COOKIES
Serves 2

ALMOND COOKIES
½ cup plus 2 tablespoons (3 oz/100 g)
blanched almonds
¼ cup (1¾ oz/ 50 g) sugar
1 small egg, beaten
½ teaspoon amaretto
or almond extract (essence)
¼ cup (1¾ oz/50 g) extra sugar,
for rolling cookies

BERRIES
½ cup (4 oz/125 g) mixed berries such as
raspberries, blueberries, strawberries
2 tablespoons confectioners' (icing) sugar
½ cup (4 fl oz/125 ml)
heavy (double) cream, whipped

Preheat oven to 350°F (180°C/Gas 4). Line a baking sheet with parchment or waxed (greaseproof) paper.

Almond Cookies: Combine the almonds and sugar in a food processor and process to a fine meal. With the machine running, add enough of the beaten egg and amaretto or almond extract (essence) so that the mixture forms a mass.

Place the mixture on a work surface and pat together until it forms a cohesive mass. Place the sugar for

PRECEDING PAGE: Pecan Tartlets
OPPOSITE: Berries in Whipped Cream with Almond Cookies

ABOVE: Coeurs à la Crème   OPPOSITE: Almond Puddings

rolling in a small bowl. Divide the dough into 3 equal parts. Roll each part into a 1-inch (2.5 cm) wide rope. Cut each rope into 6 even pieces, roll each into a ball and then roll each one in the sugar. Place the cookies 1 inch (2.5 cm) apart on the prepared baking sheet. Bake for 15 minutes, until just pale. Cool on a rack.

Berries: Cut any of the larger berries in half. Fold the confectioners' (icing) sugar into the whipped cream. Gently fold in the berries. Serve immediately with the Almond Cookies.

Any leftover cookies can be stored in an airtight container for up to 1 week.

•

COEURS À LA CRÈME

Serves 2

3 oz (90 g) cottage cheese
2 tablespoons heavy (double) cream
1 oz (30 g) cream cheese
2 tablespoons confectioners' (icing) sugar

1 tablespoon Cointreau
or other orange liqueur
Fresh fruit, for serving

Place the cottage cheese in a food processor and process until smooth. Add the cream, cream cheese and sugar and process until completely combined. Line 2 heart-shaped molds with a double thickness of dampened cheesecloth (muslin). Pack the cheese mixture into the molds. Cover with plastic wrap. Place the molds on a wire rack over a plate or bowl and refrigerate for 24 hours.

To serve, turn onto a serving plate and sprinkle with some of Cointreau. Serve with fresh fruit.

•

ALMOND PUDDINGS

Serves 2

¾ cup (6 fl oz/185 ml) milk
½ cup (1¾ oz/50 g) blanched almonds,
ground to a coarse meal
⅙ oz (5 g) gelatin
1 tablespoon water
2 tablespoons (1 oz/30 g) sugar
½ teaspoon vanilla extract (essence)
½ cup (4 fl oz/125 ml)
heavy (double) cream, whipped

Combine the milk and ground almonds in a saucepan. Place over moderate heat and bring to boiling point. Remove from the heat and set aside for 10 minutes. Strain through a fine sieve into a bowl.

Meanwhile, dissolve the gelatin in the water. Stir into the strained milk along with the sugar. Allow to cool, stirring occasionally.

Stir in the vanilla. Cover and refrigerate until the mixture begins to set, about 20 minutes. Fold in the whipped cream.

Lightly oil two 1-cup (8 fl oz/250 ml) metal molds. Pour in the pudding mixture so that they are completely full. Cover with plastic wrap and refrigerate until set, at least 2 hours. Remove the plastic wrap, unmold and serve immediately.

BUTTERSCOTCH PUDDINGS

Serves 2

PUDDINGS

1½ tablespoons (¾ oz/20g)
sweet (unsalted) butter
1 tablespoon packed brown sugar
1 small egg
½ cup plus 1 tablespoon (2 oz/60 g)
self-rising flour, sifted
¼ teaspoon baking powder
½ tablespoon instant coffee,
dissolved in 1 teaspoon boiling water
Whipped cream, for serving

BUTTERSCOTCH SAUCE

½ tablespoon (¼ oz/10 g) sweet (unsalted)
butter
⅛ cup (1 fl oz/30 ml)
light corn or golden syrup
1 tablespoon water
1 tablespoon packed brown sugar

Preheat oven to 350°F (180°C/Gas 4). Grease two 1-cup (8 fl oz/250 ml) custard cups or pudding molds and dust them with flour.

Prepare a water bath by filling a baking dish with enough water to come one-third of the way up the sides of the molds.

Puddings: Cream the butter and sugar until light and fluffy. Add the egg, slowly, beating well after each addition.

Stir in the sifted flour and baking powder. Stir in the coffee.

Spoon the mixture into the prepared molds. Tent each mold loosely, leaving a peak at the top, with buttered aluminum foil. Place the molds in the water bath and bake for 40 minutes.

Butterscotch Sauce: Place all the sauce ingredients in a pan, stirring over medium heat until the mixture is combined. Bring to a boil and boil for 3–4 minutes. The sauce should be used immediately. Serve the puddings warm with whipped cream and the Butterscotch Sauce.

OPPOSITE: Butterscotch Puddings

BUTTERSCOTCH PUDDINGS

1. Stir the coffee into the pudding mixture.

3. Tent each mold loosely, leaving a peak at the top, with buttered aluminum foil.

2. Spoon the mixture into the prepared molds.

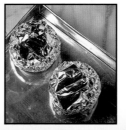
4. Place in the prepared water bath.

BUTTERMILK PUDDINGS WITH MANGO SAUCE

Serves 2

PUDDINGS
¼ cup plus 3 tablespoons
(3½ fl oz/100 ml) heavy (double) cream
½ cup (3½ oz/100 g) sugar
⅙ oz (5 g) gelatin
1 tablespoon water
½ vanilla bean
1 cup (8 fl oz/250 ml) buttermilk

MANGO SAUCE
1 mango, peeled and pitted
1 tablespoon confectioners' (icing) sugar

Puddings: Combine ¼ cup (2 fl oz/60 ml) of the cream with the sugar in a saucepan and bring to the boiling point. Remove from heat.

Dissolve the gelatin in the water. Stir into the cream mixture and mix well. Transfer to a bowl and stir in the buttermilk. Split the vanilla bean and scrape the seeds into the pudding. Refrigerate for 20 minutes, stirring occasionally.

Whip the remaining 3 tablespoons of the cream and fold into the mixture. Pour into 2 lightly oiled 1-cup (8 fl oz/250 ml) metal molds. Fill each mold right to the top. Wrap with plastic; refrigerate for 2 hours.

Mango Sauce: Place the mango flesh and sugar in a food processor. Purée. Strain through a sieve.

Unmold each pudding and serve with Mango Sauce.

ABOVE: Buttermilk Puddings with Mango Sauce
OPPOSITE: Chocolate Crunch Waffles

CHOCOLATE CRUNCH WAFFLES WITH CARAMEL SAUCE & ICE CREAM

Serves 2

CARAMEL SAUCE
⅓ cup (2 oz/60 g) brown sugar
⅓ cup (2½ fl oz/75 ml) heavy
(double) cream
4 tablespoons (2 oz/60 g)
sweet (unsalted) butter

WAFFLES
3 tablespoons (1½ oz/45 g)
butter, melted
1 oz (30 g) dark (unsweetened)
chocolate, melted
⅓ cup (2 oz/60 g) sugar
1 egg, separated
½ cup (2 oz/60 g)
all-purpose (plain) flour
1 teaspoon baking powder
¼ teaspoon salt
⅓ cup (2½ fl oz/75 ml) milk
2 tablespoons chopped walnuts
Vanilla ice cream, for serving
Chocolate shavings, for decoration

Caramel Sauce: Combine all of the sauce ingredients in a small saucepan. Stir over low heat until the sugar dissolves. Bring to a boil, reduce heat and simmer, stirring, for 3 minutes.

Waffles: Combine the melted butter and chocolate and stir vigorously until well combined. Add the sugar and egg yolk and beat well.

Sift together all the dry ingredients and add to the chocolate mixture alternately with the milk. Beat the egg white until stiff. Fold into the chocolate mixture.

Heat a waffle iron and cook the mixture according to the manufacturer's instructions. (It is best to oil the waffle iron for this mixture, as it tends to stick.) Serve immediately with the Caramel Sauce, vanilla ice cream, and shavings of chocolate.

FRUIT COBBLER
Serves 2

FILLING
2 tablespoons sugar
1½ cups (12 fl oz/375 ml) water
Zest (rind) of 1 orange, cut off in strips
6 apricots

COBBLER TOPPING
2½ cups (10 oz/315 g)
all-purpose (plain) flour
Pinch of salt
3 tablespoons packed brown sugar
½ teaspoon baking powder
2 tablespoons (1 oz/30 g)
sweet (unsalted) butter
¼ cup (2 fl oz/60 ml) light (single) cream
Extra cream, for glazing

Filling: Combine 2 tablespoons of the sugar, water and orange zest (rind) in a saucepan and stir over low heat to dissolve the sugar. Bring to a boil, add the apricots and simmer for 2–3 minutes. Remove the apricots and drain. Halve and remove the pits. Place in a baking dish that will fit the apricots in a layer 2 deep.

Preheat oven to 350°F (180°C/Gas 4).

Cobbler Topping: Combine the flour, salt, sugar, baking powder and butter in a food processor. Process to a coarse meal.

Transfer the topping to a bowl and gradually add the cream, mixing with a fork until the mixture is just combined.

Roll out the dough to about ¾ inch (2 cm) thick. Using a cookie cutter, cut the dough into shapes, such as stars or hearts. Place the shapes on top of the apricots and brush with a little extra cream. Sprinkle with the remaining 1 tablespoon of sugar. Bake for 20–25 minutes, until the top is golden brown.

Serve warm with whipped cream or ice cream.

LEFT: Fruit Cobbler

Big Bands

·

Entertain a crowd with the bold and brassy flavors of
these stylish desserts. You'll be the bandleader of a
gala gathering when you present these easy
sweet treats with swing.

CHOCOLATE-RAISIN MASCARPONE CAKE

Serves 12

1 cup (5 oz/155 g) raisins
¾ cup (6 fl oz/185 ml) brandy
8 oz (250 g) semisweet (dark) chocolate
16 tablespoons (8 oz/250 g) sweet
(unsalted) butter, at room temperature
1¾ cups (12 oz/375 g) sugar
8 eggs
1 cup (4 oz/125 g) all-purpose (plain)
flour, sifted
13 oz (410 g) mascarpone cheese
1 cup (8 fl oz/250 ml) heavy (double)
cream, whipped

Soak the raisins in the brandy until plump, at least 3 hours or overnight.

Preheat oven to 350°F (180°C/Gas 4). Butter a 9-inch (22 cm) springform cake pan.

Line the bottom of the pan with a round of parchment or waxed (greaseproof) paper.

Melt the chocolate in a double boiler over hot, not simmering, water. Set aside to cool.

Cream the butter and sugar until light and fluffy. Beat in the eggs, one at a time, beating well after each addition. Add the cooled, melted chocolate and fold in the flour. Drain the raisins, reserving the brandy, and fold them into the mixture. Pour into the prepared pan. Bake for 40 minutes, until a skewer inserted in the middle comes out clean. Let the cake cool in the pan.

When cool, remove the cake from the pan and, using a serrated knife, cut the cake horizontally in half, creating 2 cake layers.

Combine the mascarpone and whipped cream and stir in 2 tablespoons of the reserved brandy from the raisins. When the cake has completely cooled, top the bottom layer with one-third of the mascarpone mixture. Place the other layer of the cake on top and spread the remaining mascarpone over the top and sides of the cake.

Refrigerate until ready to serve, or serve immediately.

UPSIDE-DOWN LIME & MANGO SYRUP CAKE

Serves 10

3 mangoes
11 tablespoons (5½ oz/170 g) sweet
(unsalted) butter, at room temperature
¾ cup (5½ oz/170 g) sugar
3 eggs
1½ cups (5½ oz/170 g) self-rising flour
1 teaspoon baking powder
2 tablespoons grated lime zest (rind)
1 tablespoon fresh lime juice
¼ cup (1½ oz/45 g) macadamia nuts,
chopped into small pieces
Cream or ice cream, for serving

SYRUP
¼ cup (2 fl oz/60 ml) fresh lime juice
¼ cup (1¾ oz/50 g) sugar

Preheat oven to 350°F (180°C/Gas 4). Butter a 9-inch (22 cm) springform cake pan.

Peel and pit the mangoes. Cut into thin strips. Arrange the mango slices on the bottom of the pan, covering it completely.

Cream the butter and sugar until light and fluffy. Beat in the eggs, one at a time, beating well after each addition. Sift together the flour and baking powder and fold into the butter mixture alternately with the lime zest (rind), lime juice and macadamia nuts.

Pour the batter over the mango slices. Bake for 50 minutes.

Reduce heat to 300°F (150°C/Gas 2) and bake for 30 minutes more, until a skewer inserted in the middle of the cake comes out clean. Cool in the pan on a rack for 10 minutes.

Syrup: Combine the lime juice and sugar in a small nonaluminum saucepan. Stir over low heat until the sugar dissolves. Bring to a boil and boil

PREVIOUS PAGE: Chocolate-raisin Mascarpone Cake (left) and
Upside-down Lime & Mango Syrup Cake (right)
OPPOSITE : Lime Delicious

for 3–4 minutes, until the syrup thickens slightly. Invert the cake onto a serving plate and brush with the lime syrup. Serve immediately with cream or ice cream.

•

LIME DELICIOUS
Serves 12

20 tablespoons (10 oz/315 g) sweet
(unsalted) butter
3 cups (10 oz/315 g) sugar
Grated zest (rind) and juice of 8 limes
10 eggs, separated
4 cups (32 fl oz/1 l) milk
⅔ cup (2½ oz/75 g)
all-purpose (plain) flour, sifted

Preheat oven to 350°F (180°C/Gas 4). Lightly butter twelve 1-cup (8 fl oz/250 ml) ovenproof ramekins. Half-fill a baking pan large enough to hold the ramekins (if necessary, use 2 baking pans) with water. Place the pans in the oven.

Cream the butter and sugar until light and fluffy. Beat in the lime zest (rind). Beat in the egg yolks, one at a time, beating well after each addition. Fold in the milk and flour alternately with the lime juice. (If the mixture curdles, hand whisk until the mixture comes together.)

Beat the egg whites until stiff peaks form. Fold into the lime mixture. Spoon the mix-
ture into the prepared ramekins. Carefully place each ramekin into the prepared baking pan. Bake for 40 minutes, until the tops of the puddings are puffed and golden. Allow to cool slightly. Unmold on a serving platter and garnish with a little lime zest julienne.

Note: This mixture can be made in a 3-quart (3 liter) soufflé or other ovenproof dish. Increase the cooking time by 10 minutes.

OPPOSITE: Orange Chiffon Tart

ORANGE CHIFFON TART
Serves 10

PASTRY
2 cups (8 oz/250 g) all-purpose (plain)
flour
11 tablespoons (5½ oz/170 g) cold sweet
(unsalted) butter, cut into cubes
2 tablespoons sugar
2 egg yolks
1 tablespoon cold water
1 tablespoon grated orange zest (rind)
1 egg white, beaten

ORANGE FILLING
6 juice oranges
6 eggs
½ cup (3½ oz/100 g) sugar
16 tablespoons (8 oz/250 g) sweet
(unsalted) butter, cut into cubes

TOPPING
4 oranges
1 cup (6½ oz/200 g) sugar
¾ cup (6 fl oz/185 ml) water
Heavy (double) cream, for serving

Pastry: Combine the flour, butter and sugar in a food processor and process to a coarse meal. Add the egg yolks, water and orange zest (rind) and pulse until the mixture comes together. Remove from the processor and wrap in plastic wrap. Refrigerate for 30 minutes.

Preheat oven to 350°F (180°C/ Gas 4).

Roll out the pastry to line a 10-inch (25 cm) tart pan that has a removable base. Place a piece of foil, parchment or waxed (grease-proof) paper over the pastry and scatter with baking weights, dried beans or rice.

Bake for 15 minutes.

Remove the tart shell from the oven and remove the weights and paper. Brush the pastry with a little

beaten egg white and return to the oven. Bake for 10–15 minutes, until golden. Remove from the oven and allow to cool.

Orange Filling: Juice the oranges and strain the juice through a sieve to remove all of the pith.

Place in a nonaluminum saucepan with the eggs and sugar. Whisk together over low heat until the mixture thickens enough to coat the back of a wooden spoon.

Place the mixture in a food processor. With the motor running, add the butter cubes, piece by piece. When all of the butter is worked in, pour the mixture into the pastry shell. Cover with plastic wrap and refrigerate for 2 hours.

Topping: Slice the oranges as thinly as possible and remove any seeds. Combine the sugar and water in a saucepan and stir over low heat to dissolve the sugar. Bring to a boil and remove from the heat.

Using a pair of tongs, dip each slice of orange in the syrup and place on a wire rack.

Allow to cool slightly.

Remove the tart from the refrigerator, remove plastic wrap and arrange the orange slices decoratively over the top.

Serve immediately with cream.

OPPOSITE: Palmiers with Strawberries and Cream

PALMIERS WITH STRAWBERRIES & CREAM
Makes approx. 90/Serves 15

3 sheets (1 lb/500 g) puff pastry
2 eggs, beaten
½ cup (3½ oz/100 g) sugar
3 cups (1½ lb/750 g) strawberries,
for serving
Heavy (whipping) cream, for serving

Preheat oven to 350°F (180°C/Gas 4). Butter 2 or more baking sheets and line with parchment or waxed (greaseproof) paper.

Roll out six 12 x 6-inch (30 x 15 cm) rectangles of the puff pastry. Brush each with a little beaten egg and sprinkle with 1 teaspoon of sugar. One pastry sheet at a time, roll up one long edge halfway. Roll the opposite long edge so that the two meet at the middle. Roll up the remaining sheets of pastry in the same manner. Brush each with some of the beaten egg and sprinkle with more of the sugar. Using a sharp knife, cut each of the rolls into ¾-inch (2 cm) thick slices. Place each slice onto the prepared baking sheets, 1–1½ inches (3–4 cm) apart. Bake for 30 minutes, until puffed and golden. Remove to a wire rack to cool slightly.

Serve warm with strawberries and cream.

PALMIERS

1. Brush each sheet of puff pastry with a little beaten egg and sprinkle with 1 teaspoon of sugar.

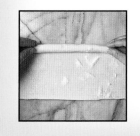

2. Roll one long edge to the middle of the pastry sheet.

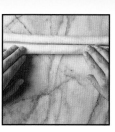

3. Roll the opposite edge so that the two meet at the middle.

4. Using a sharp knife, cut each roll into ¾-inch (2 cm) thick slices.

CARDAMOM APRICOT PUDDING
Serves 15

APRICOTS
3 lb (1½ kg) firm, ripe apricots
5 cardamom pods, bruised and tied in a
piece of cheesecloth (muslin)
One 2-inch (5 cm) cinnamon stick
1 cup (6½ oz/200 g) sugar
2 tablespoons fresh lemon juice
1½ cups (12 fl oz/375 ml) water

PUDDING
¾ cup (2½ oz/75 g) almonds
6 eggs
1 cup (6½ oz/200 g) sugar
1½ cups (6 oz/185 g) all-purpose (plain)
flour
1 teaspoon baking powder
6 tablespoons (3 oz/90 g) sweet (unsalted)
butter, melted
1 teaspoon ground cardamom
¼ cup (2 fl oz/60 ml) apricot jam
1 tablespoon water
½ cup (2 oz/60 g) sliced (flaked) almonds,
toasted
Whipped cream flavored with ground
allspice, for serving

Apricots: Halve and pit the apricots. Combine all of the other apricot ingredients in a large saucepan. Stir over low heat to dissolve the sugar. Bring to a boil. Add the apricots (it may be necessary to do the apricots in two batches, depending on the size of the saucepan) and simmer for 3 minutes. Remove to a bowl with a slotted spoon; set aside.

Pudding: Preheat oven to 350°F (180°C/Gas 4). Butter a 9 x 12 inch (22 x 30 cm) rectangular cake pan. Place the almonds in a food processor and process to a fine meal.

Beat the eggs and sugar until thick and pale.

*RIGHT: Cardamom Apricot Pudding (left) and
Pear & Almond Pudding (right)*

Sift together the flour and baking powder and fold into the egg mixture alternately with the ground almonds, melted butter and ground cardamom.

Arrange the apricot halves, cut-side down, in the base of the pan. Pour the batter over and bake for 1 hour, until a skewer inserted in the cake comes out clean. Heat together the apricot jam and water. Strain through a sieve and brush over the warm cake. Sprinkle with the toasted flaked almonds and serve warm.

Serve with the flavored whipped cream.

•

PEAR & ALMOND PUDDING
Serves 16

PEARS
1½ cups (10 oz/315 g) sugar
4 cups (32 fl oz/1 l) water
8 large pears, peeled

PUDDING
16 tablespoons (8 oz/250 g) sweet (unsalted) butter
1 cup (6½ oz/200 g) sugar
3 eggs
3½ cups (11 oz/345 g) ground almonds
2 tablespoons amaretto liqueur, or
1 teaspoon almond extract (essence)

Pears: Combine the sugar and water in a saucepan large enough to fit 4 pears. Stir over low heat to dissolve sugar, then bring to a boil. Add 4 of the pears and simmer for 5–7 minutes, until the pears are tender. Remove the pears from the syrup and set aside. Repeat with the remaining 4 pears. Bring the syrup to a boil and boil until reduced by half. Set aside.

Preheat oven to 350°F (180°C/Gas 4). Butter a

9 x 12 inch (22 x 30 cm) rectangular cake pan.

Pudding: Cream the butter and sugar until light and fluffy. Add the eggs, one at a time, beating well after each addition. Fold in the ground almonds. Add the amaretto, or the almond extract (essence) combined with 2 tablespoons of the reserved syrup.

Arrange the pears upright in the prepared pan. Spoon the filling around the base of the pears so that it comes half way up the pears. Baste each pear with a little of the reserved syrup. Bake for 45 minutes, until the almond batter is puffed and golden. Before serving, brush each pear with a little reserved syrup.

Serve warm, cutting a pear in half for each person.

•

LIME & MANGO MOUSSE WITH PASSION FRUIT SAUCE
Serves 12

LIME & MANGO MOUSSE
3 limes
¾ cup (5 oz/155 g) sugar
1 cup (8 fl oz/250 ml) water
4 envelopes (1 oz/30 g) unflavored gelatin
6 large ripe mangoes, peeled, pitted and coarsely chopped
5 oz (155 g) ricotta or mascarpone cheese

PASSION FRUIT SAUCE
8 passion fruits
¼ cup (1¾ oz/50 g) sugar

Lime & Mango Mousse: Grate the zest (rind) from 2 of the limes. Combine the zest and sugar in a saucepan over low heat. Stir to dissolve the sugar and bring to a boil. Remove from heat, and let stand for 10 minutes.

Reheat the syrup so that it is almost boiling. Dissolve

ABOVE: Lime & Mango Mousse with Passion Fruit Sauce

the gelatin in ¼ cup (2 fl oz/60 ml) of cold water set in a saucer of hot water and add to the almost-boiling syrup. Stir to combine.

Place the mangoes in a food processor and process to a purée. Add the grated zest and juice of 1 of the limes. Stir in the ricotta or mascarpone. Add the gelatin-syrup mixture and process to combine. Divide among twelve 1-cup (8 fl oz/250 ml) molds.

Cover with plastic wrap and refrigerate for at least 4 hours.

Passion Fruit Sauce: Remove the pulp from the passion fruits and place in a bowl. Stir in the sugar and allow to stand for at least 1 hour to dissolve the sugar.

Unmold the mousse on individual plates and serve with the Passion Fruit Sauce.

Folk

·

In an up-tempo world, it's comforting to know that one thing never changes — everyone still hankers after food "just like Mom used to make." And never more so than when reminiscing about her rich, homemade desserts.

LEMON MERINGUE PIE
Serves 8–10

PASTRY
2 cups (8 oz/250 g)
all-purpose (plain) flour
2 tablespoons sugar
Pinch of salt
¾ cup (6 oz/185 g)
sweet (unsalted) butter
1 tablespoon grated lemon zest (rind)
3 tablespoons lemon juice
1 tablespoon cold water
1 egg white, beaten

LEMON FILLING
Zest (rind) and juice of 2 lemons
1 cup (6½ oz/200 g) sugar
3 eggs, beaten
1 cup (8 oz/250 g) sweet (unsalted) butter

MERINGUE
6 egg whites
1 cup (6½ oz/200 g) sugar

Preheat oven to 375°F (190°C/Gas 5).

Pastry: Place the flour, sugar and salt on a work surface. Cut up the butter and rub in until the mixture resembles coarse crumbs. Add the lemon zest (rind) and enough lemon juice and water to bind the mixture. Refrigerate for 30 minutes.

Roll out the pastry large enough to line a 10-inch (25 cm) tart base. Line the pastry shell with foil, parchment or waxed (greaseproof) paper and place baking weights (dried beans or rice) on top. Bake for 20 minutes. Remove the weights and paper and brush with a little beaten egg white. Bake for another 10 minutes.

Lemon Filling: Combine the lemon zest and lemon juice, sugar and eggs in a saucepan. Stir over low heat to dissolve the sugar. Gradually add the butter in small pieces. Pour into the hot pastry shell and

OPPOSITE: Plum Crumble
PREVIOUS PAGE: Lemon Meringue Pie

place in the oven for 10 minutes, or until the filling has just set but is still a little wobbly. Let cool.

Meringue: Beat the egg whites until stiff. Gradually add 2 tablespoons of the sugar, beating constantly. Beat in the remaining sugar and continue to beat until just combined.

Reduce the heat of the oven to 300°F (150°C/Gas 2).

Pile the meringue mixture onto the cooled lemon filling and place in the oven for 10–15 minutes, or until the meringue is slightly browned. Allow to cool before slicing and serving.

●

PLUM CRUMBLE
Serves 6–8

12 dark plums
¼ cup (1¾ oz/50 g) sugar
¾ cup (6 fl oz/185 ml)
heavy (double) cream
2 tablespoons amaretto liqueur
or 1 teaspoon almond extract (essence)
(optional)

TOPPING
½ cup (3⅔ oz/105 g)
packed brown sugar
½ cup (1¾ oz/50 g)
all-purpose (plain) flour
½ cup (2½ oz/75 g) cornmeal
8 tablespoons (4 oz/125 g)
sweet (unsalted) butter

Preheat oven to 350°F (180°C/Gas 4).

Arrange the plums in a single layer in a 10 x 7-inch (24 x 18 cm) baking dish. Sprinkle with sugar. Combine the cream and amaretto and pour over the plums.

Combine the topping ingredients in a food processor and process to a coarse meal. Sprinkle over the plums.

Bake for 25–30 minutes, until the topping is golden. Serve warm with ice cream, if desired.

BREAD & BUTTER PUDDING
Serves 4–6

½ cup (2½ oz/75 g)
golden raisins (sultanas)
½ cup (1¾ oz/50 g) dried currants
⅓ cup (3 fl oz/90 ml) dark rum
8 tablespoons (4 oz/125 g)
sweet (unsalted) butter, softened
15 slices white bread or brioche loaf
5 eggs
¼ cup (1¾ oz/50 g) sugar
3½ cups (28 fl oz/875 ml) milk
1 teaspoon vanilla extract (essence)
Cream or ice cream, for serving

Soak the raisins and currants in the rum for at least 1 hour. Preheat the oven to 350°F (180°C/Gas 4). Fill a roasting pan with enough hot water to come halfway up the side of the 1-quart (1 liter) baking dish you plan to use for the pudding. Place it in the oven. Butter the baking dish. Butter the bread or brioche slices. Cut into triangles and arrange in the dish, alternately with the raisins and currants, until all are used.

In a bowl, whisk together the eggs and sugar until pale. Heat the milk to boiling point and whisk into the egg mixture. Add any remaining rum and the vanilla. Pour over the bread and let stand for 10 minutes to allow it to soak up the egg custard. Place the dish in the roasting pan in the oven and cook for 40–45

minutes, or until the custard is just set. If the top browns too quickly, place aluminum foil over the top to prevent burning.

Serve warm with cream or ice cream.

•

RICE PUDDING
Serves 4

1 (½ oz/10 g)
envelope unflavored gelatin
3 tablespoons cold water
3 cups (24 fl oz/750 ml) milk
3 tablespoons short-grain white rice
1½ tablespoons sugar
1 cup (8 fl oz/250 ml)
heavy (double) cream
1 teaspoon vanilla extract (essence)

ABOVE: Rice Pudding   OPPOSITE: Bread & Butter Pudding

Soak the gelatin in the cold water, set over a saucer of warm water, until dissolved.

Meanwhile, place 2 cups (16 fl oz/500 ml) of the milk in a saucepan, add the rice and cook, stirring often, over moderate heat for 20 minutes, until the rice is tender. Add the dissolved gelatin and stir. Add the remaining 1 cup (8 fl oz/250 ml) of milk and the sugar and stir to dissolve. Remove from the heat and allow to cool.

Whip the cream until soft peaks form, add the vanilla and then fold into the rice mixture. Place in a serving bowl and chill. Serve with fresh fruit, if desired.

BERRY SHORTCAKE
Serves 8

2 cups (8 oz/250 g)
all-purpose (plain) flour, sifted
2 teaspoons baking powder
¼ teaspoon salt
2 tablespoons sugar
10 tablespoons (5 oz/155 g)
butter, cut into pieces
⅔ cup (5½ fl oz/170 ml) milk

BERRY CREAM
2½ cups (20 fl oz/600 ml)
heavy (double) cream
3 cups (24 oz/750 g) berries
4 tablespoons sugar

Preheat the oven to 400°F (200°C/Gas 6). Grease an 8-inch (22 cm) round cake pan or baking dish. In a food processor, combine the flour, baking powder, salt and sugar. Add the butter and process the mixture to a coarse meal. Add some of the milk and continue to process until the mixture just comes together.

Turn the dough onto a floured surface and gently knead to a smooth ball. Gently pat the dough into the prepared pan and bake for 15 minutes, until the shortcake is slightly puffed and golden. Remove from the oven and allow to cool slightly. Unmold using 2 forks. Split the shortcake in two, horizontally.

Berry Cream: Whip the cream to soft peaks. Process one-third of the berries with the sugar to a purée. Strain the purée through a fine sieve into the cream. Beat the cream mixture until stiff.

Top each shortcake with the Berry Cream and decorate with the remaining fresh berries.

RIGHT: Berry Shortcake

SHORTBREAD COOKIES
Makes 20

16 tablespoons (8 oz/250 g) butter
½ cup (1½ oz/45 g)
confectioners' (icing) sugar, sifted
1⅔ cups (6 oz/185 g)
all-purpose (plain) flour, sifted
¼ cup (1 oz/30 g) rice flour, sifted*

ICING
½ cup (1½ oz/45 g)
confectioners' (icing) sugar
1 tablespoon water
Few drops of red or yellow food coloring

Preheat the oven to 275°F (140°C/Gas 1). Lightly grease a baking sheet.

Beat together the butter and confectioners' (icing) sugar until the mixture is light and fluffy. Using a wooden spoon, stir in the combined flours. Pat the dough into a ball, wrap in plastic wrap and refrigerate for 30 minutes.

Working on a lightly floured surface, roll out the dough to about ½ inch (1¼ cm) thick. Cut out cookie shapes, using cookie cutters. Place on the prepared baking sheet and bake for 25–30 minutes, or until the cookies look set and lightly browned. Cool on a wire rack.

Icing: Combine the confectioners' sugar with enough of the water to make a smooth paste. Add a drop of food coloring and mix into the paste. Using a pastry (piping) bag, pipe some of the icing around the edges of the cookies. Leave for about 5–10 minutes to set.

Note: The cookies can be kept, stored in an airtight container, for up to 1 week.

*If rice flour is unavailable, all-purpose (plain) flour can be used instead.

ABOVE: Shortbread Cookies
OPPOSITE: Baked Cheesecake

BAKED CHEESECAKE
Serves 8–10

CRUST
8 oz (250 g) graham crackers
(sweet biscuits)
13 tablespoons (6½ oz/200 g)
sweet (unsalted) butter, melted

1½ cups, plus 2 tablespoons (13 oz/375 g)
cream cheese
1½ cups, plus 2 tablespoons (13 oz/375 g)
ricotta cheese
1 cup (7 oz/200 g) sugar
3 eggs
2 tablespoons all-purpose (plain) flour
1½ cups (12 fl oz/375 ml) sour cream
1 tablespoon lemon juice
1 tablespoon grated lemon zest (rind)

Preheat the oven to 300°F (150°C/Gas 2).

Crust: Grind the graham crackers (sweet biscuits) in a food processor to fine crumbs. Place in a mixing bowl. Pour the melted butter over the crumbs, and stir to combine. Press into an 8-inch (20 cm) springform pan, lining the base and sides.

Place the cream cheese, ricotta cheese and sugar in a food processor and process until smooth. (Alternatively you can use an electric mixer.) Add the eggs, 1 at a time, mixing well after each addition. Transfer to a bowl (if using a processor) and fold in the flour, sour cream, lemon juice and lemon zest (rind). Pour into the crust-lined pan. Bake for 1 hour, or until the cheesecake is set in the middle. Turn off the heat and leave in the oven for another 15 minutes, with the door ajar. Remove from the oven and set aside to cool completely. Refrigerate for at least 2 hours before serving.

T R I F L E
Serves 6

**1 package (3 oz/90 g)
orange or cherry gelatin (jelly crystals)
1 (10 inch/25 cm) sponge cake
⅓ cup (2½ fl oz/85 ml) fruit jelly (jam)
½ cup (4 fl oz/125 ml) sweet sherry
1 cup (8 oz/250 g) blueberries
4 apricots, pitted and cut into eighths***
Extra fruit, for decoration

**PASTRY CREAM
6 egg yolks
½ cup (3½ oz/100 g) sugar
3 tablespoons all-purpose (plain) flour
2 cups (16 fl oz/500 ml) milk
1 teaspoon vanilla extract (essence)
1 cup (8 fl oz/250 ml) heavy (double)
cream, whipped**

Make the gelatin (jelly crystals) according to the directions on the package. Chill in the refrigerator for at least 1 hour, until set.

Cut the cake horizontally into 3 layers and spread 1 side of each layer with the jelly (jam). Sandwich the layers back together and then cut into cubes or fingers and sprinkle with the sherry. Set aside until needed.

Make the pastry cream as shown below.

To assemble the trifle, arrange one-third of the cake pieces on the bottom of a 1-quart (1 liter) bowl. Top with one-third of the gelatin and fruits and one-third of the pastry cream mixture. Repeat these layers, finishing with a pastry cream layer and decorating with the extra fruit.

Refrigerate for at least 2 hours. The trifle is best left overnight before serving.

*With the exception of pineapple, any fruits in season can be used in the layers of the trifle.

P A S T R Y   C R E A M

1. Whisk the egg yolks and sugar until thick and pale. Whisk in the flour.

3. Cook the pastry cream over low heat, whisking constantly, until the mixture thickens. Remove from heat and cool. Stir in the vanilla.

2. Strain the milk into the egg yolk mixture. Whisk until the pastry cream is smooth and has no lumps.

4. Fold the pastry cream into the lightly whipped cream.

OPPOSITE: Trifle

GINGERBREAD WITH PINEAPPLE CREAM
Serves 6

6 tablespoons (3 oz/90 g)
sweet (unsalted) butter
¼ cup (2 fl oz/60 ml) milk
½ cup (4 fl oz/125 ml) sour cream
1 egg
½ cup (4 oz/125 g) brown sugar
¾ cup (3 oz/90 g)
all-purpose (plain) flour
1 teaspoon baking powder
2 teaspoons ground ginger
1 teaspoon ground cinnamon
½ teaspoon ground cloves
½ teaspoon ground cardamom
2 tablespoons finely chopped almonds
2 tablespoons chopped crystallized ginger
Fresh mint leaves, for decoration

PINEAPPLE CREAM
¼ medium-size pineapple
Approx. 2 tablespoons sugar
(to taste, depending on the
sweetness of the pineapple)
2 cups (16 fl oz/500 ml)
heavy (double) cream

ABOVE: *Baked Stuffed Apples*
OPPOSITE: *Gingerbread with Pineapple Cream*

Preheat the oven to 350°F (180°C/Gas 4). Grease an 8-inch (20 cm) square cake pan.

Put the butter and milk in a saucepan and heat until the butter melts. Set aside to cool. When cooled, stir in the sour cream, then stir in the egg and brown sugar and whisk until smooth.

Sift the flour and baking powder into a large bowl and add the ginger, cinnamon, cloves, cardamom and almonds. Make a well in the center and pour in the milk mixture. Stir until smooth and then stir in the crystallized ginger. Pour the mixture into the prepared pan. Bake for 25–30 minutes, or until a skewer inserted in the middle comes out clean.

Pineapple Cream: Finely chop the pineapple (using a food processor, if preferred). Drain and sprinkle with sugar. Whip the cream to soft peaks. Fold in the pineapple. Serve immediately.

Serve the Gingerbread warm with the Pineapple Cream and decorated with mint, if desired.

•

BAKED STUFFED APPLES
Serves 6

2 cups (16 fl oz/500 ml) water
1½ cups (11 oz/345 g)
packed brown sugar
2 cinnamon sticks
6 medium-size Granny Smith
(or other green) apples
¾ cup (4 oz/125 g)
golden raisins (sultanas)
½ cup (2 oz/60 g) hazelnuts, chopped
Grated zest (rind) of 1 orange
2 tablespoons brandy
4 tablespoons (2 oz/60 g)
sweet (unsalted) butter

Preheat oven to 375°F (190°C/Gas 5).

Combine the water and 1 cup (7 oz/220 g) of the brown sugar in a saucepan. Stir over low heat to dissolve the sugar. Add the cinnamon sticks and bring to a boil. Boil for 3 minutes. Set aside.

Remove the apple cores without cutting all the way

to the bottom. Mix the remaining brown sugar, golden raisins (sultanas), hazelnuts and orange zest (rind) together. Fill each apple with this mixture, so that each is three-fourths full. Drizzle a little brandy into each and dot with butter. Place the apples in a baking dish and pour on the brown sugar syrup. Basting occasionally, bake for 30 minutes, until tender.

Transfer the apples to a serving dish and the syrup to a saucepan. Boil and reduce the syrup by one-third. Pour the syrup over the apples and serve.

•

BAKED CUSTARD
Serves 8

3 whole eggs
2 egg yolks
½ cup (3½ oz/100 g) sugar
3 cups (24 fl oz/750 ml) milk
1 teaspoon vanilla extract (essence)
¼ teaspoon freshly grated nutmeg

Preheat oven to 165°F (325°C/Gas 3).

Butter a 1-quart (1 liter) baking dish and place it in a roasting pan which has enough hot water to come halfway up the side of the baking dish. Place in the oven to heat.

Combine the eggs, egg yolks and sugar, and whisk until thick and pale.

Heat the milk to boiling point and slowly add to the egg mixture, stirring constantly. Stir in the vanilla. Strain through a sieve into the baking dish and sprinkle with nutmeg. Place in the roasting pan and bake for 45 minutes, until set.

The custard is set when a knife inserted in the center comes out clean.

OPPOSITE: Baked Custard

Fanfare

Here is finale fare with a flourish, a crescendo of desserts that will have both neophyte fans and those with sophisticated palates standing to applaud. Parade these treats past a crowd and enjoy the resounding chords of appreciation.

FRUIT & CHOCOLATE BRANDY CAKE

Serves 10–12

CAKE

½ cup (1¾ oz/50 g) glacéed apricots
½ cup (1¾ oz/50 g) dried figs
½ cup (1¾ oz/50 g) dried prunes
⅓ cup (1¾ oz/50 g) glacéed cherries
⅓ cup (1¾ oz/50 g) glacéed ginger
¼ cup (2 fl oz/60 ml), plus 2 tablespoons
brandy or dark rum
8 tablespoons (4 oz/125 g) sweet
(unsalted) butter
10 oz (315 g) semisweet (dark)
chocolate, chopped
½ cup (3½ oz/100 g) sugar
2 eggs, separated
½ cup (4 fl oz/125 ml) sour cream
1 cup (3½ oz/100 g)
all-purpose (plain) flour
1 teaspoon baking powder
⅔ cup (2 oz/60 g) ground almonds

ICING

6½ oz (200 g) semisweet (dark)
chocolate, chopped
1 tablespoon light olive oil
Silver balls, for decorating

Cake: Finely chop the fruits and place in a bowl with ¼ cup (2 fl oz/60 ml) of the brandy or rum. Set aside for 2–3 hours.

Preheat oven to 300°F (150°C/Gas 2). Butter an 8-inch (20 cm) round cake pan and line with waxed (greaseproof) paper.

Melt the butter and 8 oz (250 g) of the chocolate in a double boiler. Remove from heat and stir in the remaining brandy or rum and whisk in the egg yolks, 1 at a time. Stir in the sour cream.

Sift the flour and baking powder together and fold into the mixture alternately with the ground almonds. Beat the egg whites until stiff peaks form. Fold one-third of the egg whites into the mixture. Fold in the fruits and any remaining brandy or rum

and the remaining 2 oz (60 g) of chopped chocolate, and then fold in the remaining egg whites. Pour into the prepared pan. Bake for 1½ hours, until a skewer inserted in the middle comes out barely moist. Let cool in the pan for 15 minutes. Invert onto a wire rack to cool completely.

Icing: Melt the chocolate in a double boiler. Just before the chocolate completely melts, stir in the oil. Continue to stir until smooth. Allow to cool. With the cake on the wire rack, pour the icing over the cake; use a metal spatula to spread it evenly over the top and sides. Decorate with silver balls and leave to set for 15 minutes before serving.

•

STICKY DATE PUDDING WITH CARAMEL SAUCE

Serves 8–10

STICKY DATE PUDDING

1½ cups (8 oz/250 g)
pitted, chopped dates
1½ cups (12 fl oz/375 ml) water
1 teaspoon baking soda
(bicarbonate of soda)
4 tablespoons (2 oz/60 g)
sweet (unsalted) butter
¾ cup (5 oz/155 g) sugar
2 eggs
1 cup (4 oz/125 g)
self-rising flour, sifted
Heavy (double) cream, for serving

CARAMEL SAUCE

1 cup (5 oz/155 g) packed brown sugar
1 cup (8 fl oz/250 ml)
heavy (double) cream
13 tablespoons (6½ oz/200 g) sweet
(unsalted) butter

*PREVIOUS PAGE: Sticky Date Pudding with Caramel Sauce
(left) and Fruit & Chocolate Brandy Cake (right)*
OPPOSITE: Peanut Brittle Florentines with Chocolate Ice Cream

Preheat oven to 350°F (180°C/Gas 4). Butter a 9-inch (22 cm) springform cake pan and line with parchment or waxed (greaseproof) paper.

Sticky Date Pudding: Combine the dates and water in a medium saucepan and bring to a boil. Remove from heat and stir in the baking soda (bicarbonate of soda). Place three-fourths of the dates in a food processor and purée. Set aside. Cream the butter and sugar. Beat in the eggs, 1 at a time, beating well after each addition. Fold in the sifted flour, the puréed dates and the remaining chopped dates. Pour the mixture into the prepared pan. Bake for 55 minutes, or until a skewer inserted in the middle comes out clean.

Caramel Sauce: Combine all of the sauce ingredients in a small saucepan. Stir over low heat until the sugar dissolves and the butter melts. Continue to stir for another 3 minutes, until combined and warm.

Let the pudding stand for 10 minutes before unmolding onto a serving platter. Serve immediately with the Caramel Sauce and cream.

•

PEANUT BRITTLE FLORENTINES WITH CHOCOLATE ICE CREAM
Serves 8

ICE CREAM
8 egg yolks
¾ cup (5 oz/155 g) sugar
4 cups (32 fl oz/1 l) milk
2 cups (16 fl oz/500 ml) heavy (double) cream
11 oz (345 g) semisweet (dark) chocolate, melted and cooled

FLORENTINES
3 tablespoons (1½ oz/45 g) sweet (unsalted) butter

2 tablespoons honey
¼ cup (2 oz/60 g) packed brown sugar
¼ cup (¾ oz/20 g) all-purpose (plain) flour, sifted
¼ cup (1½ oz/45 g) peanuts, chopped
¼ cup (1 oz/30 g) glacéed cherries, chopped
3½ oz (100 g) semisweet (dark) chocolate, melted

Ice Cream: Combine the egg yolks and granulated sugar and beat until thick and creamy. Place the milk and cream in a saucepan and bring to boiling point. Remove from the heat and whisk gradually into the egg yolk mixture. Return the mixture to the saucepan and cook, stirring, over low heat until the mixture thickens and coats the back of a wooden spoon. Set aside to cool for 15 minutes.

When cool, fold in the melted chocolate. Transfer to an ice cream machine and freeze according to manufacturer's instructions.

Florentines: Preheat oven to 350°F (180°C/Gas 4). Line 2 baking sheets with parchment or waxed (greaseproof) paper.

Place the butter, honey and brown sugar in a saucepan and bring to a boil. Remove from the heat and let cool. Stir in the flour, peanuts and cherries. Drop 2 teaspoonfuls of the mixture 2 inches (5 cm) apart onto the prepared baking sheets and cook for 12–15 minutes, until golden. Remove from the oven and let cool for 5 minutes on the baking sheets. Carefully remove the florentines to a wire rack to cool completely.

When completely cool, spread the smoothest side of each florentine with some of the melted chocolate. When the chocolate is almost set, make a pattern using the tines of a fork. Let set completely. Serve the Peanut Brittle Florentines with the Chocolate Ice Cream.

Individual Caramel Fruit Puddings

INDIVIDUAL CARAMEL FRUIT PUDDINGS

Serves 4

FRUIT PUDDINGS

½ cup (2½ oz/75 g)
dried apricots, chopped
⅓ cup (1¾ oz/50 g)
pitted prunes, chopped
½ cup (2½ oz/75 g) **dried figs, chopped**
¼ cup (1¾ oz/50 g) **currants**
½ cup (4 fl oz/125 ml) **dark rum**
2 (1¾ lb/800 g) **brioche loaves**
12 tablespoons (6 oz/185 g)
sweet (unsalted) butter
½ cup (2½ oz/75 g) **packed brown sugar**
Whipped cream, for serving
Light (single) cream, for serving
Toffee Swirls (page 155), for decorating

CARAMEL SAUCE

1½ cups (12 oz/375 g) **sugar**
½ cup (4 fl oz/125 ml) **water**
2 cups (16 fl oz/500 ml) **heavy (double) cream**

Fruit Puddings: Combine the dried fruits in a bowl. Pour the rum over the fruits and let stand for 3 hours. Preheat oven to 350°F (180°C/Gas 4).

Remove the crusts and then cut the brioche into strips to line the sides of four ¾-cup (6 fl oz/185ml) pudding molds. Cut circles from the bread to fit the bottom and the top of each mold.

Cream the butter and sugar until pale and fluffy. Use this mixture to spread on both sides of the brioche strips and circles. Place 1 circle on the bottom of each mold and cover the sides with the strips. Fill with the fruit and liquid. Top with a brioche circle.

Bake for 15–20 minutes, until the tops are crisp and browned. Run a knife around the edge of each mold.

Caramel Sauce: Combine the sugar and water in a saucepan. Stir over low heat to dissolve the sugar, bring to a boil and boil until the syrup turns a golden color. Remove from heat and quickly stir in the cream. If the mixture is not smooth, return briefly to low heat and stir until any lumps dissolve.

Cover 4 plates half with caramel sauce and half cream. Swirl some of the caramel sauce through the cream. Unmold the puddings and place each on a plate, top with whipped cream and decorate with Toffee Swirls.

CHOCOLATE TRUFFLE TART
Serves 10–12

PASTRY
1¾ cups (6½ oz/200 g) all-purpose (plain) flour
2 teaspoons sugar
8 tablespoons (4 oz/125 g) sweet (unsalted) butter
1 egg yolk
3 tablespoons ice water

CHOCOLATE LAYER
12 tablespoons (6 oz/185 g) sweet (unsalted) butter
½ cup (3½ oz/100 g) sugar
6 eggs
1¼ lb (600 g) semisweet (dark) chocolate, melted and cooled
¼ cup (2 fl oz/60 ml) light (single) cream
1 teaspoon vanilla extract (essence)

TRUFFLES
5½ oz (170 g) semisweet (dark) chocolate, finely chopped
⅔ cup (5½ fl oz/170 ml) heavy (double) cream
1 tablespoon (½ oz/15 g) sweet (unsalted) butter
½ cup (1½ oz/45 g) unsweetened cocoa powder

Pastry: Place the flour and sugar in a food processor. Pulse to combine. Add the butter and process until the mixture resembles coarse crumbs. Add the egg yolk and then the water a little at a time, pulsing until the mixture just comes together. Pat into a ball. Wrap in plastic wrap and refrigerate for 30 minutes.

Roll out the pastry and fit into a 10-inch (27 cm) tart pan. Refrigerate for 30 minutes.

Preheat oven to 400°F (200°C/Gas 6).

LEFT: Chocolate Truffle Tart

Line the pastry with a sheet of aluminum foil, weigh down with baking weights, dried beans or rice. Bake the pastry shell for 10 minutes. Reduce the temperature to 350°F (180°C/Gas 4) and bake for another 10 minutes. Remove the foil and weights and bake for 10 minutes more, until the pastry is golden. Allow to cool completely.

Chocolate Layer: Cream the butter and sugar until fluffy. Beat in the eggs, 1 at a time, beating well after each addition. Continue beating for another 2 minutes, until the mixture has lightened and increased in volume. Whisk in the cooled chocolate. Stir in the cream and vanilla. Pour into the cooled pastry shell and refrigerate for at least 6 hours.

Truffles: Place the chocolate pieces in a bowl. Combine the cream and butter in a saucepan and bring to boiling point. Pour this mixture over the chocolate and stir until smooth. Set aside to cool. Cover and refrigerate until the mixture is hard enough to roll into balls, about 40 minutes.

Dust your hands with a little cocoa powder and roll teaspoonfuls of the mixture into balls. Roll the balls in some more cocoa and leave in a cool place.

Just before serving, remove from the refrigerator and decorate with the Truffles.

Preheat oven to 350°F (180°C/Gas 4).

Macaroons: Place the hazelnuts on a baking tray and roast for 10 minutes. Remove from the oven, and process to a fine meal. Sift the confectioners' (icing) sugar and baking soda (bicarbonate of soda), add the ground hazelnuts and mix well.

Turn the oven down to 250°F (130°C/Gas ½). Line a baking sheet with waxed (greaseproof) paper.

Beat the egg whites until stiff, fold in the hazelnut mixture.

Using a pastry (piping) bag, pipe about twelve 3-inch (8 cm) rounds of mixture onto the prepared baking sheet. Bake for 5 minutes. Reduce oven to 225°F (110°C/Gas ¼) and bake for another 35 minutes. Set aside to cool.

Filling: Divide the mascarpone into 2 bowls. Add the chocolate syrup to 1 bowl and stir to combine. Add the coffee and 2 teaspoons of confectioners' sugar to the other and stir to combine.

Using a pastry (piping) bag, pipe a layer of chocolate mascarpone mixture onto one-third of the macaroons. Top each with another macaroon and pipe on a layer of coffee mascarpone mixture. Top each with a third macaroon and dust with confectioners' sugar to serve.

•

HAZELNUT MACAROONS
Serves 4

MACAROONS
½ cup (3 oz/90 g) whole hazelnuts
1 cup (6 oz/185 g) confectioners'
(icing) sugar
¼ teaspoon baking soda
(bicarbonate of soda)
2 egg whites

FILLING
1 lb (500 g) mascarpone cheese
¼ cup (2 fl oz/60 ml) chocolate syrup
2 tablespoons instant coffee
2 teaspoons confectioners' (icing) sugar,
plus extra for dusting

•

MACADAMIA NUT CAKES
Serves 4

4 eggs
¾ cup (5 oz/155 g) sugar
1 cup (4 oz/125 g) all-purpose (plain) flour
4 tablespoons coarsely chopped
macadamia nuts
4 tablespoons (2 oz/60 g) sweet (unsalted)
butter, melted and cooled
¾ cup (6 oz/185 ml) heavy
(double) cream, whipped
½ teaspoon vanilla extract (essence)
½ cup (1¾ oz/50 g) shredded (desiccated)
coconut, lightly toasted

OPPOSITE: Hazelnut Macaroons

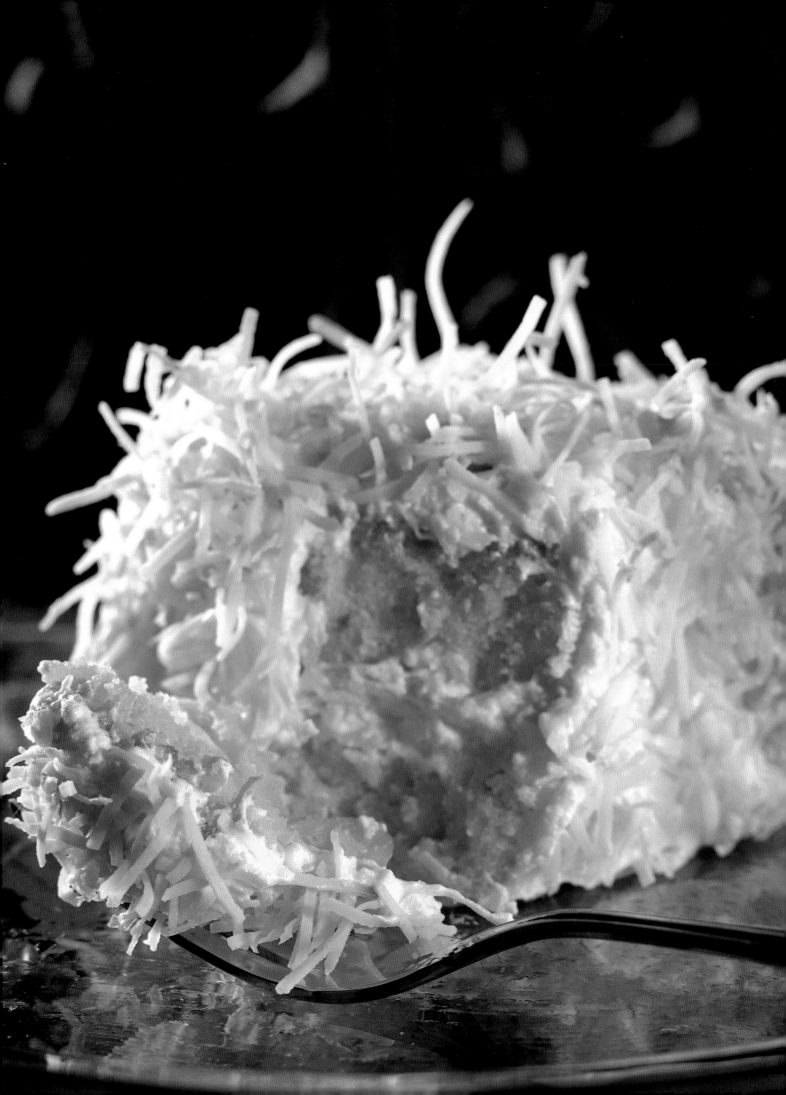

ABOVE: *Plum Clafoutis*   OPPOSITE: *Macadamia Nut Cakes*

Preheat oven to 350°F (180°C/Gas 4). Butter and line an 8-inch (20 cm) square cake pan.

Combine the eggs and sugar in a large bowl and beat until the sugar dissolves and the mixture is thick and creamy, 5–7 minutes. Sift half the flour into the egg mixture and gently fold in. Repeat with the remaining flour and 2 tablespoons of the macadamia nuts. Carefully and quickly fold in the butter. Pour the mixture into the prepared pan. Bake for 20 minutes, until the cake feels springy to the touch.

Invert the cake onto a wire rack to cool completely. When cool, cut into 4 squares. Cut each square horizontally in half.

Combine the remaining 2 tablespoons of macadamia nuts, whipped cream and vanilla in a bowl. Spread the bottom half of each square with a little of the cream mixture. Place the other half on top and spread the remaining cream over the top and edges. Sprinkle all over with the toasted shredded (desiccated) coconut. Serve immediately.

PLUM CLAFOUTIS
Serves 6

7 tablespoons (3½ oz/100g)
sweet (unsalted) butter
6 firm, ripe plums
¾ cup (3 oz/90 g) all-purpose
(plain) flour, sifted
1 cup (3½ oz/100g) ground almonds
1 cup (7 oz/220 g) sugar
1 teaspoon baking powder
3 eggs
1 cup (8 fl oz/250 ml) milk
Whipped cream, for serving

Preheat oven to 350°F (180°C/Gas 4).

Butter a 9 x 5 x 3-inch (23 x 13 x 8 cm) loaf pan.

Place the butter in a small saucepan and cook over moderate heat until golden, almost brown in color. Set aside to cool until needed.

Halve the plums and remove the pits. Arrange the

plum halves, cut-side up, over the bottom of the prepared loaf pan.

Combine all of the dry ingredients in a large bowl and make a well in the center. Beat together the eggs and milk and stir into the dry ingredients. Fold the browned butter into the batter.

Pour the batter over the plums. Bake for 40–45 minutes, until the cake feels firm to the touch and a skewer inserted in the middle comes out barely moist.

Serve with whipped cream.

•

TOFFEE FIGS WITH CHAMPAGNE SABAYON

Serves 4

TOFFEE FIGS
1 cup (7 oz/220 g) sugar
½ cup (4 fl oz/125 ml) water
8 small fresh figs

CHAMPAGNE SABAYON
4 egg yolks
⅓ cup (2 oz/60 g) sugar
½ cup (4 fl oz/125 ml)
champagne or sparkling white wine

Toffee Figs: Place the sugar and water in a saucepan and cook over low heat, stirring until the sugar dissolves. Bring to a boil and cook, without stirring, until golden, 5–8 minutes. Remove from heat. Holding the stalks of the figs, dip each in the toffee, swirling to coat all sides. Plunge into ice water for a few seconds to harden the toffee. Remove to a serving platter. It is important to work quickly as the toffee will harden.

Champagne Sabayon: Combine all of the sabayon ingredients in the top of a double boiler or a round-bottomed metal bowl. Whisk to combine. Set over hot, not boiling, water and cook, whisking until light and thick, at least 5 minutes. Serve warm.

Serve the Toffee Figs in bowls with the Champagne Sabayon.

OPPOSITE: Toffee Figs with Champagne Sabayon

TOFFEE FIGS

1. Place the sugar and water in a saucepan and cook over low heat to dissolve the sugar.

3. Holding the stalks of the figs, dip each in toffee, swirling to coat all sides.

2. Bring to a boil and cook until golden, about 5–8 minutes.

4. Plunge each fig into ice water for a few seconds to harden the toffee.

CHOCOLATE BROWNIES WITH ICE CREAM & CHOCOLATE SAUCE

Serves 4

CHOCOLATE BROWNIES
16 tablespoons (8 oz/250 g)
sweet (unsalted) butter
2 cups (14 oz/440 g) sugar
4 eggs, lightly beaten
½ cup (1½ oz/45 g) unsweetened
cocoa powder
2 teaspoons vanilla extract (essence)
⅔ cup (2½ oz/75 g) all-purpose
(plain) flour, sifted
13 oz (410 g) semisweet (dark) chocolate,
chopped into small pieces
½ cup (2 oz/60 g) toasted hazelnuts
4 cups (32 fl oz/1 l) vanilla ice cream

CHOCOLATE SAUCE
½ cup (4 fl oz/125 ml) cream
6½ oz (185 g) semisweet (dark)
chocolate, cut into small pieces

Preheat oven to 350°F (180°C/Gas 4). Lightly butter an 8-inch (20 cm) square cake pan.

Chocolate Brownies: Melt the butter in a saucepan over low heat. Remove from heat and stir in the sugar, eggs, cocoa powder, flour and vanilla. Add the chopped chocolate and hazelnuts. Pour into the prepared pan and bake for 40–45 minutes, until a toothpick inserted in the center comes out clean. Cool completely in pan.

Chocolate Sauce: Heat the cream until it is just about to boil. Remove from the heat and add the chocolate. Let stand for 10 minutes before stirring until smooth.

When cool, remove the brownies from the pan and cut into 8 rectangles. To serve, slice the ice cream into 4 rectangles, the size of each brownie. Place between 2 brownies and serve immediately with Chocolate Sauce on top.

RIGHT: Chocolate Brownies

"Rap"

Between these pastry and crêpe "wraps" is a flavorful sensation waiting to be discovered. These desserts will have guests and family singing their praises in quick time. For an alternative treat, pick up the beat — try these surprise sweets!

APRICOTS IN CREAM CHEESE PASTRY

Serves 4

½ cup (3½ oz/100 g) dried apricots
1 tablespoon brandy
1 tablespoon fresh orange juice
Grated zest (rind) of ½ orange
2 tablespoons sugar

PASTRY

8 oz (250 g) cream cheese,
at room temperature
16 tablespoons (8 oz/250 g) sweet
(unsalted) butter
¼ cup (2 fl oz/60 ml)
light (single) cream
2 tablespoons sugar
Pinch of salt
2½ cups (10 oz/315 g) all-purpose
(plain) flour
1 egg, beaten
Light (single) cream, for serving

Combine the apricots, brandy, orange juice, orange zest (rind) and sugar in a nonaluminum saucepan and stir over low heat for 5 minutes. Remove from heat and allow to cool completely. Preheat oven to 350°F (180°C/Gas 4). Line a baking sheet with parchment or waxed (greaseproof) paper.

Pastry: Place the cream cheese, butter, cream and sugar in a food processor and beat until smooth. Add the salt and flour and stir until combined. Pat the dough into a ball, cover with plastic wrap and refrigerate for 1 hour.

Roll out the dough and cut into eight 4-inch (10 cm) circles. Place 2 teaspoons of the apricot mixture in the middle of each circle and pinch together to make 4 sides, like an open, square-based pyramid. Brush the outside of the pastry with a little beaten egg, and place on the prepared baking sheet. Bake for 20 minutes, until golden.

Serve warm, with cream.

ALMOND PITHIVIERS

Makes 12

¾ cup (3 oz/90 g) whole almonds
¼ cup (1 oz/30 g)
all-purpose (plain) flour
10 tablespoons (5 oz/155 g) sweet
(unsalted) butter, at room temperature
¾ cup (2½ oz/75 g) confectioners'
(icing) sugar
1 egg
1 lb 6 oz (670 g) puff pastry (page 154)
1 egg, beaten
Whipped cream, for serving

Place the almonds and flour in a food processor and process to a fine meal.

Cream the butter and sugar, add the almond mixture and mix until combined. Add the egg and beat until combined.

Roll out the puff pastry ¼ inch (6 mm) thick. Cut out six 2½-inch (6 cm) circles and six 4-inch (10 cm) circles.

Line a baking sheet with parchment or waxed (greaseproof) paper and butter the paper.

Place a little almond mixture in the center of a smaller circle and brush the edges with a little beaten egg. Gently place a larger circle over the top, and gently press the edges together to seal. Set the pithiviers on the prepared baking sheet and refrigerate for 30 minutes.

Preheat the oven to 350°F (180°C/Gas 4). (Remove the top oven rack to allow the pastry to rise as it bakes.)

Using a knife, score a criss-cross pattern on the top of each pithivier; do not cut completely through the pastry. Brush each pithivier with a little of the beaten egg.

Bake on the center rack for 15–20 minutes, until golden brown. Remove from oven and cool on a wire rack. Serve warm with whipped cream.

*PREVIOUS PAGE: Almond Pithiviers (left) and
Apricots in Cream Cheese Pastry (right)
OPPOSITE: Cherry Strudel*

CHERRY STRUDEL

Serves 6

FILLING
1 can (1¼ lb/600 g) tart pitted cherries
1 tablespoon kirsch liqueur
2 tablespoons sugar
½ teaspoon ground cinnamon
1 teaspoon cornstarch (cornflour)
dissolved in 1 tablespoon water

4 tablespoons (2 oz/60 g) sweet (unsalted) butter, melted
8 sheets filo pastry
Heavy (double) cream, for serving

Filling: Place the cherries and ¼ cup (2 fl oz/60 ml) of their liquid in a nonaluminum medium saucepan. Add the kirsch, sugar, cinnamon and cornstarch (cornflour) mixture. Cook over medium heat, stirring constantly, until the mixture thickens and boils. Set aside to cool, about 30 minutes.

Place a piece of foil on a large baking sheet and brush with a little of the melted butter. Place 1 sheet of filo onto the baking sheet. Brush with melted butter and place a second sheet of filo over the first, and brush with melted butter. Repeat with all 8 sheets of the pastry. Spread the filling over the pastry, leaving a 1-inch (2.5 cm) margin on the long edges and a 2-inch (5 cm) margin on the short edges.

Fold the short edges in and loosely roll the pastry into a roll. Place the strudel, seam-side down, in the center of the baking sheet and brush the top with melted butter. Bake for 25 minutes, until the strudel is puffed and golden.

Slice and serve immediately, drizzled with the heavy (double) cream.

POPPY SEED CRÊPES WITH STRAWBERRIES & CREAM
Serves 6

CRÊPES
4 eggs
¼ cup (1¾ oz/50 g) sugar
1 cup (8 fl oz/250 ml) milk
1 cup (4 oz/125 g) all-purpose (plain)
flour, sifted
4 tablespoons (4 oz/60 g) sweet
(unsalted) butter, melted
1 tablespoon poppy seeds

VANILLA CREAM
1 cup (8 fl oz/250 ml) heavy (double)
cream, whipped
1 teaspoon vanilla extract (essence)
2 tablespoons confectioners' (icing) sugar
2 cups (8 oz/250 g) hulled strawberries
Heavy (double) cream, for serving

Crêpes: Place the eggs in a large bowl. Beat in the sugar, milk, flour, 2 tablespoons of the melted butter and the poppy seeds. Cover and stand for 30 minutes.
Vanilla Cream: Combine all of the ingredients in a bowl and mix well.

Heat a crêpe pan or nonstick frying pan over moderate heat. Brush the bottom with some of the remaining melted butter. Pour 2 tablespoons of the crêpe mixture into the pan and tilt to spread evenly and thinly. Cook for 2–3 minutes, until the top is just set and the bottom is golden brown. Turn over and cook other side for about 1 minute. Remove to a plate.

Repeat until all of the mixture is used, making at least 6 crêpes.

Stack the crêpes, with a piece of parchment or waxed (greaseproof) paper between each crêpe. Keep the whole plate covered with a clean dish towel.

When all of the crêpes are cooked, place 1 tablespoon of the Vanilla Cream on the edge of each crêpe. Roll into a thin roll and turn the ends in to form a circle shape. Top each crêpe with some of the hulled strawberries and drizzle with some of the cream.

WINTER FRUIT PIE
Serves 8

3 dried pear halves
½ cup (3½ oz/100 g) dried figs
½ cup (3½ oz/100 g) prunes
¼ cup (1¾ oz/50 g) raisins
¼ cup (2 oz/60 g) currants
½ cup (1½ oz/50 g) dried apricots
Zest (rind) of 1 orange
½ cup (4 fl oz/125 ml)
dark rum, whisky or brandy
1 apple, peeled, cored and sliced
1 pear, peeled, cored and sliced
1 teaspoon ground allspice
¼ cup (1¾ oz/75 g) sugar
4 tablespoons (2 oz/60 g)
sweet (unsalted) butter
11 oz (345 g) puff pastry (page 154)
1 egg, beaten
Heavy (double) cream, for serving

Chop the dried fruit and soak in alcohol for 24 hours. Preheat oven to 350°F (180°C/Gas 4).

Place the pear and apple in a medium saucepan and sprinkle with the sugar and allspice. Add the butter and cook over low heat until the fruit is tender, about 10 minutes. Remove from heat and set aside.

Roll out half of the puff pastry to a thickness of ⅛ inch (3 mm) and use to line the base of a 9-inch (22 cm) pie dish, leaving an overhang of 1 inch (2.5 cm). Line with parchment or waxed (greaseproof) paper and cover with baking weights, dried beans or rice. Bake for 15 minutes. Remove from the oven and remove the weights and paper.

Fill the pie with layers of apples and pears and drained dried fruits. Roll out the remaining puff pastry ⅛ inch (3 mm) thick, place over the pie and pinch the pastry edges together. Brush with beaten egg and make a small incision in the top. Bake for 25–30 minutes, until puffed and golden. Serve warm with cream.

PREVIOUS PAGE: Winter Fruit Pie (left) and
Poppy Seed Crêpes with Strawberries & Cream (right)
OPPOSITE: Individual Raisin & Citrus Peel Pies

INDIVIDUAL RAISIN & CITRUS PEEL PIES
Makes 18

PASTRY
2 cups (8 oz/250 g) all-purpose (plain) flour
½ teaspoon salt
12 tablespoons (6 oz/185 g) sweet (unsalted) cold butter
⅓ cup (2½ fl oz/75 ml) cold water
1 egg, beaten

FILLING
½ cup (2¾ oz/80 g) chopped raisins
¼ cup (1⅓ oz/40 g) mixed candied citrus peel
2 tablespoons honey
4 tablespoons (2 oz/60 g) sweet (unsalted) butter, melted
¼ cup (2½ oz/75 g) packed brown sugar
Whipped cream, flavored with 1 teaspoon ground allspice, for serving

Pastry: Mix together the flour and salt. Rub in the butter until the mixture resembles coarse breadcrumbs. Slowly add the water, a tablespoon at a time, mixing with your fingertips, until the pastry comes together. Press gently into a ball. Wrap in plastic wrap and refrigerate for 30 minutes.

Filling: Mix together the raisins, citrus peel, honey, brown sugar and butter.

Preheat the oven to 400°F (200°C/Gas 6).

Roll out the pastry to a thickness of ⅓ inch (¾ cm). Cut out thirty-six 2-inch (5 cm) rounds. Do this in batches, keeping the prepared circles under a clean dish towel.

Place 1 teaspoon of the filling in the center of 18 of the pastry rounds. Moisten the edges with a little milk or beaten egg and place a round of pastry over each filled round. Seal the edges with the tines of a fork and cut a small incision in the top of each. Place on a lightly greased baking sheet and bake for 10–15 minutes, until golden. Serve warm with whipped cream flavored with 1 teaspoon of ground allspice.

•

FILO NUT PASTRIES
Serves 4

1 cup (3½ oz/100 g) mixed hazelnuts, pecans and walnuts
2 tablespoons honey
1 tablespoon (½ oz/15 g) sweet (unsalted) butter
1 teaspoon ground allspice
3 sheets filo pastry
2 tablespoons (1 oz/30 g) sweet (unsalted) butter, melted
Confectioners' (icing) sugar, for dusting
Cream or ice cream, for serving

Preheat oven to 350°F (180°C/Gas 4). Line a baking sheet with parchment or waxed (greaseproof) paper and butter it.

Place the nuts in a food processor and process to a coarse meal. Combine the honey and butter in a small saucepan and stir over low heat until combined. Add to the processor with the allspice and process to combine.

Brush each sheet of filo with melted butter, layering one on top of the other. Cut the layered sheet lengthwise into 4 strips. Place 2 teaspoons of the nut mixture on one corner of each strip and fold diagonally across. Continue to fold backwards and forwards diagonally across the entire pastry strip. (You should end up with a triangular packet.) Brush each packet with a little more melted butter and place on the baking sheet. Bake for 15–20 minutes, or until the packets are puffed and golden. Sprinkle with confectioners' (icing) sugar and serve with cream or ice cream.

OPPOSITE: Filo Nut Pastries

CHOCOLATE CRÊPES WITH MASCARPONE & TOFFEE

Serves 6

CRÊPES
2 eggs
¼ cup (1¾ oz/50 g) sugar
1 cup (8 fl oz/250 ml) milk
½ cup (1¾ oz/50 g) all-purpose
(plain) flour, sifted
1 tablespoon unsweetened cocoa powder
Pinch of salt
3 tablespoons (1½ oz/45 g) sweet
(unsalted) butter, melted

TOFFEE
1 cup (7 oz/220 g) sugar
1 cup (8 fl oz/250 ml) water
8 oz (250 g) mascarpone cheese

CHOCOLATE SAUCE
5 oz (155 g) semisweet (dark) chocolate
2 tablespoons (1 oz/30 g)
sweet (unsalted) butter
½ cup (4 fl oz/125 ml) heavy
(double) cream
1 tablespoon brandy, if desired

Crêpes: Place the eggs in a large bowl and beat well. Beat in the sugar, milk, flour, cocoa powder, salt and 2 tablespoons of the melted butter. Cover and let stand for 30 minutes.

Toffee: Combine the sugar and water in a saucepan. Stir over low heat until the sugar dissolves. Bring to a boil and boil until golden, 5–7 minutes. Lightly oil a baking sheet. Pour the toffee onto the sheet and tilt so that the toffee forms a thin layer. Let cool and harden for 10 minutes.

Remove the toffee pieces from the baking sheet, place in a bowl and crush the toffee with a spoon. Stir three-fourths of the crushed toffee into the mascarpone. Set aside the remainder for decoration.

Chocolate Sauce: Melt the chocolate and butter over simmering water in a double boiler. Stir in the cream until completely blended. Flavor with the brandy, if desired.

Heat a crêpe pan or 8-inch (20 cm) nonstick frying pan over moderate heat. Brush the bottom of the pan with some of the remaining 1 tablespoon of melted butter. Pour in 2 tablespoons of the crêpe batter and tilt the pan to spread the batter evenly and thinly. Cook for 2–3 minutes until the crêpe is just set on top and brown underneath. Turn to the other side and cook for 1 minute. Remove to a plate and repeat until all of the mixture is used, making at least 6 crêpes.

CHOCOLATE CRÊPES

1. Beat the sugar, milk, flour, cocoa powder, salt and 2 tablespoons of the melted butter into the eggs.

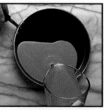

3. Pour in 2 tablespoons of the crêpe batter and tilt the pan to spread the batter evenly and thinly.

2. Brush the bottom of the pan with some of the remaining 1 tablespoon of melted butter.

4. Cook for 2-3 minutes until the crêpe is just set on top and brown underneath. Turn to the other side and cook for 1 minute.

Chocolate Crêpes with Mascarpone & Toffee

Stack the cooked crêpes on a plate with a piece of parchment or waxed (greaseproof) paper between each crêpe. Keep the whole plate covered with a clean dish towel.

When all of the crêpes are cooked, place 1 tablespoon of mascarpone and toffee mixture in the center of each crêpe. Fold the sides over so that it looks like a pillow.

Serve each crêpe drizzled with chocolate sauce and extra toffee.

Country

•

Take your partner...and do-se-do out to the heart of
the country. Loll by a stream, dangle a line, and feast
on perfect picnic fare. Then round it all off with
sweet somethings.

INDIVIDUAL ALMOND TARTS
Makes 6

PASTRY
2 cups (8 oz/250 g) all-purpose
(plain) flour
2 teaspoons sugar
10 tablespoons (5 oz/155g)
cold sweet (unsalted) butter
1 egg yolk
2 tablespoons ice water
1 egg white, beaten

FILLING
4 tablespoons (2 oz/60g)
sweet (unsalted) butter
⅓ cup (2 oz/60 g) sugar
1 egg
1 cup (3½ oz/100g) ground almonds
1 teaspoon almond extract (essence)
2 tablespoons berry jelly or jam

Pastry: Combine the flour, sugar and butter in a food processor. Process to a coarse meal. Pulse the machine and add the egg yolk and enough of the ice water to form a cohesive mass. Remove the dough, wrap in plastic wrap and refrigerate for 30 minutes. Preheat oven to 300 F (150° C/Gas 2).

Roll out the pastry to ⅓-inch (¾ cm) thick. Cut into six 3-inch (8 cm) circles. Line a 6-cup cupcake pan with the pastry circles and brush each with a little beaten egg white. Refrigerate for 30 minutes. Line each pastry circle with a round of foil, parchment or waxed (greaseproof) paper and place baking weights (dried beans or rice) in the center of each. Bake for 10 minutes.

Remove from the oven and remove the weights and foil or paper, Let cool.

Filling: Cream the butter and sugar until fluffy. Add the egg and beat well. Fold in the ground almonds and almond extract (essence). Spread each pastry shell with about ½ teaspoon of jelly or jam and top with the almond filling. Bake for 10–15 minutes, until the filling is puffed and

golden. Cool for 10 minutes in the pan; unmold and cool on a rack. Serve at room temperature.

•

APPLE & DATE CAKE
Serves 8–10

CAKE
2 green apples
1 cup (6 oz/185 g) chopped, pitted dates
1 teaspoon baking
soda (bicarbonate of soda)
1 cup (8 fl oz/250 ml) boiling water
8 tablespoons (4 oz/125 g) sweet
(unsalted) butter
1 cup (6½ oz/200 g) sugar
1 egg
1½ cups (6 oz/185 g) all-purpose
(plain) flour

TOPPING
4 tablespoons (2 oz/60 g) sweet
(unsalted) butter
½ cup (3½ oz/100 g) brown sugar
½ cup (1¾ oz/50 g) shredded coconut

Preheat oven to 350°F (180°C/Gas 4). Grease and line a 9-inch (23 cm) springform pan.

Cake: Peel and core the apples and chop into small pieces. Combine the apples, dates, baking soda (bicarbonate of soda) and boiling water. Let cool. Cream the butter and sugar until pale. Beat in the egg. Fold in the flour alternately with the apple and date mixture. Pour into the prepared pan. Bake for 50 minutes.

Topping: Place all of the topping ingredients in a saucepan and stir over moderate heat until the butter melts and the ingredients are combined.

Pour the topping over the cake and return it to the oven. Bake until the topping is bubbling and golden, about 15 minutes more.

OPPOSITE: Individual Almond Tarts
PREVIOUS PAGE: Apple & Date Cake

SWEET APPLE PIZZA
Serves 10–12

PIZZA DOUGH
1 tablespoon sugar
1 cup (8 fl oz/250 ml) lukewarm water
1 envelope (¼ oz/7 g) active dry yeast
3½ cups (14 oz/440 g)
all-purpose (plain) flour
¼ cup (2 fl oz/60 ml) light olive oil

APPLESAUCE
4 large green apples,
peeled, cored and coarsely chopped
2 tablespoons fresh lemon juice
1 cup (7 oz/220 g) sugar

TOPPING
5 large green apples
2 tablespoons fresh lemon juice
½ cup (3½ oz/100 g) sugar
½ teaspoon ground cinnamon
7 tablespoons (3½ oz/100 g)
sweet (unsalted) butter
¼ cup (2 fl oz/60 ml) apricot jelly or jam
½ cup (1¾ oz/50 g) ground almonds

Pizza Dough: Dissolve the sugar in lukewarm water. Sprinkle on the yeast and stir until dissolved. Leave in a warm place for 5–10 minutes, until the mixture starts to bubble.

Sift the flour into a large bowl and make a well in the center. Pour in the oil and the yeast mixture and, using a metal fork or spatula, stir the liquid, slowly incorporating the flour. When the dough forms a mass, turn onto a lightly floured surface and begin to knead. If the dough is too sticky, add more flour. Knead for 10 minutes, until the dough feels elastic and smooth.

Lightly grease a bowl with a little oil and place the dough in the bowl. Cover with plastic wrap and leave in a warm place until doubled in bulk, about 1–1½ hours.

Remove the dough from the bowl and punch down. Knead and shape into a ball. Re-oil the bowl and

return the dough. Cover and set aside for 30 minutes.

Applesauce: Combine all of the ingredients in a saucepan and cook over low heat until the apples are soft, about 10 minutes. Mash the apples with a fork and set aside.

Topping: Peel and core the apples and cut into thin slices. Combine the lemon juice, sugar, cinnamon and 6 tablespoons of the butter in a large frying pan. Cook over low heat until the butter melts. Add the apple slices in a single layer and cook over low heat for 2–3 minutes. Set aside to cool slightly. Combine the apricot jelly or jam and the remaining 1 tablespoon of butter in a small saucepan and cook over low heat, stirring until the butter has melted. Preheat oven to 500°F (250°C/Gas 10). Lightly oil 2 baking sheets. Remove the dough from the bowl and divide into four equal parts. Roll out each piece of dough into an oval and place on a baking sheet. To assemble: Spread each oval of dough with one-fourth of the Applesauce. Arrange the apple slices on top. Using a pastry brush, brush each pizza with a little of the apricot mixture. Sprinkle with the ground almonds. Bake for 10 minutes. Reduce the heat to 350°F (180°C/Gas 4) and bake for 10 minutes, until the edges of the pizzas are golden. Serve warm, or at room temperature.

●

STOLLEN
WITH BERRY JAM
Makes 1 large or 2 small loaves

STOLLEN
1 cup (8 fl oz/250 ml) milk
½ cup (3½ oz/100 g) sugar
1 teaspoon salt
11 tablespoons (5½ oz/170 g) butter,
melted and cooled
1 envelope (¼ oz/7 g) active dry yeast
2 tablespoons warm water
4 cups (1 lb/500 g) all-purpose (plain) flour
2 eggs, beaten

OPPOSITE: Sweet Apple Pizza

½ cup (2 oz/60 g)
chopped, blanched almonds
½ cup (2½ oz/75 g) chopped golden raisins
(sultanas)
¼ cup (2 oz/60 g) currants
¼ cup (2 oz/60 g) chopped candied
citrus peel
2 tablespoons chopped candied cherries
Grated zest (rind) of 1 lemon
1 teaspoon vanilla extract (essence)
2 tablespoons (1 oz/30 g) melted butter, for
top of bread
2 tablespoons sugar, for top of bread

BERRY JAM
2 cups (16 oz/500 g) fresh or frozen
mixed berries
½ cup (3½ oz/100 g) sugar
1 teaspoon lemon juice

Stollen: Heat the milk to boiling point and stir in the sugar, salt and butter until melted. Cool to lukewarm. Dissolve the yeast in the warm water and add to the cooled milk mixture with 1 cup (4 oz/125 g) of the flour. Set aside to rest in a warm place until the mixture bubbles, about 10 minutes.

Stir in the eggs and remaining 3 cups (12 oz/375 g) of flour until a light, sticky dough forms. Knead in the chopped nuts, fruit, peel and zest (rind) and continue to knead until the mixture is smooth and elastic, about 5 minutes. Cover the dough lightly with a clean linen dish towel and set aside in a warm place to rise until doubled in bulk, about 1 hour.

Punch down the dough and let it rest for 10 minutes. Flatten into an oval (or divide the dough and flatten into 2 ovals). Brush the top with the melted butter and sprinkle with the sugar. Fold the loaf, lengthwise, almost in half and pinch the ends together firmly. Place on an oiled baking sheet and brush with a little more melted butter. Set aside to rise for 1 hour, until doubled in bulk.

Preheat oven to 425°F (220°C/Gas 7). Bake for 10 minutes. Reduce the temperature to 350°F (180°C/Gas 4) and bake for another 40 minutes, until the loaf is golden and sounds hollow when tapped.

Berry Jam: Combine all of the ingredients in a saucepan and cook over low heat for 3–4 minutes, gently stirring, until the juices start to run from the berries and the sugar has dissolved. Cool.

Serve the Stollen sliced, spread with butter and some of the Berry Jam.

ABOVE: Stollen with Berry Jam
OPPOSITE: Plum Compote with Rich Almond Cake

PLUM COMPOTE WITH RICH ALMOND CAKE
Serves 4–6

PLUM COMPOTE
1 cup (8 fl oz/250 ml) dry red wine
¼ cup (2 fl oz/60 ml) honey
Juice and julienned zest (rind) of 1 orange
1½ lb (750 g) whole plums

RICH ALMOND CAKE
8 tablespoons (4 oz/125 g)
sweet (unsalted) butter
¾ cup (5 oz/155 g) sugar
3 eggs
¾ cup (3 oz/90 g) ground almonds
⅓ cup (1½ oz/45 g)
all-purpose (plain) flour
2–3 drops almond extract (essence)
Confectioners' (icing) sugar, for dusting

Plum Compote: Place the wine in a saucepan and boil until reduced by half. Add the honey and stir to dissolve. Stir in the orange juice and zest (rind).

Add the plums. Reduce the heat and simmer, stirring occasionally, for 2–3 minutes.

Place the fruit in a bowl and allow to cool completely.

Rich Almond Cake: Preheat oven to 350°F(180°C/Gas 4). Grease and line an 8-inch (20 cm) round cake pan.

Cream the butter and sugar. Add the eggs, one at a time, beating well after each addition. Fold in the ground almonds, flour and almond extract (essence) one-third at a time. Pour the batter into the prepared pan and bake for 45–50 minutes, or until a skewer inserted in the center comes out clean. The cake should shrink slightly from the edges of the pan. Turn the cake out onto a wire rack to cool. Dust with confectioners' (icing) sugar.

Serve slices of the cake in a bowl, together with 2 or 3 plums per serving.

•

CARAMEL & ALMOND FUDGE
Makes 64 squares

**2¾ cups (1¾ lb/800 g)
packed brown sugar
2 cups (16 fl oz/500 ml)
heavy (double) cream
Pinch of salt
1⅔ cups (6½ oz/200 g)
chopped almonds**

Line an 8-inch (20 cm) square pan with waxed (greaseproof) paper or plastic wrap.

Place the sugar, cream and salt in a large saucepan and cook, stirring, over low heat, until the sugar melts. Bring to boiling point and cook, without stirring, until the mixture reaches the soft ball stage.* If crystals form on the edge of the pan, brush them off with warm water, using a pastry brush. Let the mixture cool (to 110°F [45°C] if using a thermometer).

RIGHT: Chocolate Mint Sandwich Cookies (left) and Caramel and Almond Fudge (right)

Transfer to a bowl and beat until the fudge is thick and creamy, about 5 minutes. Stir in the chopped almonds and pour into the prepared pan. Refrigerate for 2 hours. Cut into 1–1½-inch (2–3 cm) squares.

*The soft ball stage is reached when a little of the mixture, dropped in cold water, forms a cohesive but still soft ball. If using a thermometer, the mixture should be 236–238°F (113–114°C).

•

CHOCOLATE MINT SANDWICH COOKIES
Makes 12 cookies

COOKIES
½ cup (2 oz/60 g) all-purpose (plain) flour
½ cup (2 oz/60 g) self-rising flour
¼ cup (½ oz/15 g)
confectioners' (icing) sugar
½ cup (2¾ oz/80 g) semisweet (dark)
chocolate, or chocolate chips, melted
1 egg, beaten

PEPPERMINT FILLING
1 cup (3 oz/90 g)
confectioners' (icing) sugar, sifted
1 teaspoon peppermint extract (essence)
2–3 tablespoons water

Preheat oven to 350°F (180°C/Gas 4). Line a baking sheet with parchment or waxed (greaseproof) paper.

Cookies: Sift together the flours and sugar. Combine the melted chocolate and beaten egg and pour over the flour mixture, stirring constantly with a wooden spoon to blend. Pat the mixture into a ball, wrap in plastic wrap and refrigerate for 15 minutes. Roll out the cookie dough between 2 pieces of waxed (greaseproof) paper to a thickness of ⅛ inch (3 mm). Using a star-shaped cutter, cut out 24 stars. Place on the prepared baking sheet about 1 inch (2.cm) apart. Bake for 10 minutes. Remove

OPPOSITE: Lemon & Blueberry Buckle

from the sheet and cool on a wire rack.

Peppermint Filling: Combine the sifted sugar and peppermint and enough water to make a smooth paste. (Add the water gradually, a tablespoon at a time.) Place a little on one cookie and sandwich another cookie on top. Repeat until all of the cookies are sandwiched.

•

LEMON & BLUEBERRY BUCKLE
Serves 10–12

BATTER
16 tablespoons (8 oz/250 g)
sweet (unsalted) butter
⅓ cup (2 oz/60 g) sugar
1 egg
1 tablespoon grated lemon zest (rind)
1¼ cups (5 oz/155 g)
all-purpose (plain) flour
1 teaspoon baking powder
1 teaspoon baking soda
(bicarbonate of soda)
1 cup (8 fl oz/250 ml) buttermilk
2½ cups (1 lb/500 g) blueberries
¾ cup (2½ oz/75 g) ground pecans
Crème fraîche, for serving

TOPPING
½ cup (3½ oz/100g) packed brown sugar
½ cup (4 oz/125 g)
all-purpose (plain) flour
½ cup (2 oz/60 g) pecan pieces
8 tablespoons (4 oz/125 g) sweet
(unsalted) butter, cut in pieces
1 tablespoon grated lemon zest (rind)

Preheat oven to 350°F (180°C/Gas 4). Grease a 10-inch (25 cm) round cake pan.

Batter: Cream the butter and sugar. Add the egg and mix well. Add the lemon zest (rind) and beat. Sift together the flour, baking powder and baking soda (bicarbonate of soda). Add one-third of the

flour mixture to the butter mixture and mix well. Add one-third of the ground pecans and one-third of the buttermilk and mix well. Alternately add the remaining flour, buttermilk and pecans.

Spread the batter into the prepared pan and cover with the blueberries.

Topping: Combine the brown sugar, flour and pecans in a processor. Process to a coarse meal. Add the butter and lemon zest and process for 10 seconds.

ABOVE: Cherry Pie OPPOSITE: Dried Fruit Tart

Sprinkle the crumb topping over the blueberries. Cook for 1½ hours, until a skewer inserted in the middle comes out clean. Serve with crème fraîche.

•

and water and pulse the processor until the pastry just comes together. Remove from processor and gently pat into a ball. Wrap in plastic wrap and refrigerate for at least 30 minutes.

Pie Filling: Gently mix the cherries with the sugar and kirsch and let stand for 30 minutes. Roll out the pastry and line a 10-inch (25 cm) pie pan, leaving an overhang of about 1 inch (2.5 cm). Brush the base with a little of the beaten egg white and, using a slotted spoon, put the cherries into the pastry. Discard the liquid from the cherries. Fold in the overhanging pastry and crimp the edges. Bake for 5 minutes. Reduce the oven to 350°F (180°C/Gas 4) and bake until the pastry is golden, about 25 minutes.

•

CHERRY PIE
Makes one 10-inch (25 cm) pie

PASTRY
2 cups (1 lb/500 g)
all-purpose (plain) flour
12 tablespoons (5½ oz/170 g)
sweet (unsalted) butter
2 tablespoons sugar
1 egg
1 tablespoon ice water
1 egg white, lightly beaten

PIE FILLING
2 cups (16 oz/500 g)
stemmed, pitted, tart cherries
½ cup (3½ oz/100 g) sugar
1 tablespoon kirsch liqueur

Pastry: Place the flour, butter and sugar in a food processor and process to a coarse meal. Add the egg

DRIED FRUIT TART
Serves 8–10

PASTRY
1½ cups (6 oz/185 g)
all-purpose (plain) flour
½ cup (1¾ oz/50 g) ground hazelnuts
2 tablespoons sugar
11 tablespoons (5½ oz/170 g)
sweet (unsalted) butter
1 egg
1 tablespoon cold water
Beaten egg, for glazing

FILLING
1 cup (7 oz/220 g) pitted prunes
1 cup (4 oz/125 g) dried apricots
1 large green apple,
peeled, cored and chopped
½ cup (2½ oz/75 g) raisins

½ cup (3½ oz/100 g) sugar
½ cup (2 oz/60 g) chopped walnuts
4 tablespoons (2 oz/60 g)
sweet (unsalted) butter, melted
½ cup (4 fl oz/125 ml) brandy

Pastry: Combine the flour, ground hazelnuts, sugar and butter in a food processor. Process to a coarse meal. Add the egg and water and process until the mixture just forms a mass. Gently pat together into a ball and wrap in plastic wrap. Refrigerate for 30 minutes.

Preheat oven to 350°F (180°C/Gas 4).

Filling: Combine the prunes, apricots, apple and raisins in a saucepan. Add enough water to cover and simmer until the fruit is tender, about 20 minutes.

Drain the fruit and return it to the saucepan. Add the sugar, walnuts, melted butter and brandy. Simmer for 5 minutes. Cool.

Roll out two-thirds of the pastry and line a 10-inch (25 cm) pie pan, leaving a ½-inch (1.25 cm) overhang. Spoon in the filling, piling into the center. Roll out the remaining pastry and cut into narrow strips. Arrange the strips in a lattice pattern over the top of the pie. Fold in the edge of the crust and crimp. Brush with a little beaten egg. Bake until the top is golden, about 30–35 minutes.

COCONUT CUPCAKES

Makes about 24

4 eggs
⅔ cup (4½ oz/140 g) sugar
1¼ cups (4 oz/125 g)
all-purpose (plain) flour
1 teaspoon baking powder
¾ cup (2½ oz/75 g)
flaked (desiccated) coconut
8 tablespoons (4 oz/125 g)
sweet (unsalted) butter, melted

Grease two 12-cup cupcake pans, or fit the cups with paper liners.

Combine the eggs and sugar in a large bowl. Beat until the mixture is thick and pale, and forms a ribbon.

Sift the flour with the baking powder and fold into the egg mixture alternately with the coconut, folding in the melted butter with the last batch. Chill for 25 minutes, or until the mixture thickens slightly.

Meanwhile, preheat oven to 450°F (220°C/Gas 7). Divide the mixture among the cupcake pans, filling them two-thirds full. Bake for 5 minutes. Reduce the oven temperature to 400°F (200°C/Gas 6) and bake for 5–7 minutes, or until risen and golden. Remove from oven and cool.

COCONUT BATTER

1. Combine the eggs and sugar in a large bowl and begin to whisk.

2. Beat the eggs and sugar until the mixture is thick and pale and the mixture "ribbons."

3. Fold the flour into the egg mixture, alternating it with the flaked coconut.

4. Fold the melted butter into the mixture with the last batch of coconut.

OPPOSITE: Coconut Cupcakes

Impromptu

·

Unexpected guests? A spontaneous get-together segues
into a sweet surprise for everyone when you improvise
with these innovative recipes that do a smooth take on
the basics and are a snap to present with style.

PEAR & NUT TART

Serves 4

PASTRY

1 cup (5 oz/155 g) roasted
hazelnuts, skins removed
½ cup (2 oz/60 g)
all-purpose (plain) flour
1 tablespoon packed brown sugar
2 tablespoons (1 oz/30 g)
sweet (unsalted) butter, melted
1 egg yolk

FILLING

10 oz (315 g) mascarpone cheese
1 (28 oz/820 g) can pear halves, drained
2 oz (60 g) semisweet (dark) chocolate,
melted

Preheat oven to 350°F (180°C/Gas 4).

Pastry: Place the hazelnuts in a food processor and process until fine. Add the flour and sugar and process to combine. Add the butter and the egg yolk. Process until the mixture forms a mass. Do not overprocess.

Press the pastry into an 8-inch (20 cm) round springform pan. Prick the bottom with the tines of a fork. Bake for 25 minutes, until golden. Remove from the oven and allow to cool.

Filing: When the pastry shell has cooled, fill with the mascarpone and top with the pears. Drizzle with the melted chocolate.

•

DRIED FRUITS WITH RICOTTA & BRIOCHE

Serves 6

8 oz (250 g) brioche
4 tablespoons (2 oz/60 g)
sweet (unsalted) butter, melted
½ cup (2 oz/60 g) sugar
½ cup (4 fl oz/125 ml) water
Zest (rind) of 1 orange, cut into julienne

13 oz (410 g) ricotta cheese
¾ cup (6½ oz/200 g) mixed dried fruit
(apricots, currants or raisins), chopped
¾ cup (6 fl oz/185 ml)
homemade or store-bought caramel sauce
Confectioners' (icing) sugar,
for serving (optional)

Preheat oven to 400°F (200°C/Gas 6).

Cut the brioche into twelve ½-inch (1 cm) thick slices and brush each side with a little melted butter. Place the slices on a baking sheet and bake for 10 minutes, until golden.

Heat the sugar and water in a small saucepan and stir over low heat to dissolve the sugar. Bring to a boil and boil for 3 minutes, reduce the heat and add the orange zest (rind). Simmer for 2–3 minutes. Remove the zest with a slotted spoon and set aside. Spread the ricotta on half of the toasted brioche slices, top with dried fruit, orange zest, 1–2 tablespoons of caramel sauce and another slice of toasted brioche. Sprinkle with confectioners' (icing) sugar if desired.

•

PEACH PUDDING CAKE

Serves 6–8

4 eggs
⅔ cup (4½ oz/140 g) sugar
¾ cup plus 2 tablespoons (3½ oz/100 g)
self-rising flour, sifted
¼ cup (1 oz/30 g) ground almonds
4 tablespoons (2 oz/60 g) butter, melted
1 teaspoon vanilla extract (essence)
1 (1¾ lb/800g) can peach halves, drained
Cream or ice cream, for serving

GLAZE

2 tablespoons apricot jelly or jam
1 tablespoon water

OPPOSITE: Dried Fruits with Ricotta and Brioche
PREVIOUS PAGE: Pear & Nut Tart

Preheat oven to 350°F (180°C/Gas 4). Grease a 9-inch (23 cm) springform pan.

Beat together the eggs and sugar until thick and pale. Combine the flour, baking powder and ground almonds and fold into the egg mixture in 3 batches. Add the butter and vanilla with the last batch. Pour the mixture into the prepared pan and arrange the peaches on top. Bake until a skewer inserted in the middle comes out clean, about 45–50 minutes. Cool slightly before removing from the pan.

Glaze: Combine the apricot jelly or jam and water in a saucepan and cook over low heat until blended. Brush the cake with the glaze and serve warm, with cream or ice cream.

•

LEMON CURD CUSTARDS

Serves 4

Grated zest (rind) and juice of 2 lemons
4 eggs
⅓ cup (2 oz/60 g) sugar
8 tablespoons (4 oz/125 g)
sweet (unsalted) butter, cut into small pieces
Toasted, buttered brioche, for serving

Combine the lemon zest (rind) (reserving a little for garnish), lemon juice, eggs and sugar in the top of a double boiler. Cook, stirring constantly, for 5–7 minutes over medium heat, until thick and pale.

Place the mixture in a food processor. With the motor running, gradually add the butter pieces.

Pour into four 6-ounce (9 cm diameter)

ABOVE: Lemon Curd Custard   OPPOSITE: Peach Pudding Cake

ramekins and refrigerate for at least 30 minutes. Garnish with the reserved lemon zest and serve with toasted, buttered brioche, cut into shapes.

•

CARAMELIZED PEACHES WITH VANILLA CUSTARD

Serves 4

¾ cup (5 oz/155 g) sugar
2 cups (16 fl oz/500 ml) water
4 firm ripe white or yellow peaches
1¼ cups (10 fl oz/315 ml)
store-bought or homemade custard
¾ cup plus 2 tablespoons
(6½ fl oz/200 ml) light (single) cream
1 teaspoon vanilla extract (essence)
Extra sugar, for broiling (grilling)

Combine the sugar and water in a saucepan and stir over low heat to dissolve the sugar. Bring mixture to a boil. Add the peaches and poach for 10–15 minutes, until a skewer inserted in the thickest part of the peach meets no resistance. Remove the peaches, peel off the skins and set aside. Bring the poaching syrup to a boil and boil until reduced by half, about 10 minutes. Set aside to cool slightly. Combine the custard with the cream, vanilla and 2 tablespoons of the syrup. Place the custard mixture in a bowl and place the peaches in the mixture. Sprinkle the peaches with a little extra sugar. Broil (grill) the peaches, about 2 inches (5 cm) away from the heat, until the sugar caramelizes, about 3 minutes.

MADELEINES
Makes 24

4 eggs
¾ cup (5 oz/155 g) sugar
1 cup (4 oz/125 g)
all-purpose (plain) flour, sifted
1 teaspoon baking powder
8 tablespoons (4 oz/125 g) sweet (unsalted)
butter, melted and slightly cooled
Confectioners' (icing) sugar, for dusting
Fresh fruit, for serving
Whipped cream, for serving

Combine the eggs and sugar and beat until pale and thick. Fold in the sifted flour and baking powder in 3 batches, adding the butter with the last batch. Cover and refrigerate the batter for 10 minutes. Preheat oven to 425°F (220°C/Gas 7). Brush the indentations of a madeleine pan with melted butter. Spoon the batter into the pan, filling each indentation two-thirds full. Bake for 5 minutes. Reduce heat to 400°F (200°C/Gas 6) and bake for another 5 minutes, until each cake has a small peak in the middle and they feel spongy to touch. Transfer to a wire rack to cool slightly. Serve dusted with confectioners' (icing) sugar with fresh fruit and whipped cream.

•

RASPBERRY CREAM
Serves 6

1 (½ oz/15 g) envelope
unflavored gelatin
1 cup (8 fl oz/250 ml) warm water
3 cups (1½ lb/750 g) fresh or
frozen raspberries
½ cup (3½ oz/100 g) sugar
2½ cups (20 fl oz/700 ml)
heavy (double) cream
Raspberries, extra, for decorating

Dissolve the gelatin in the warm water. Set aside ½ cup (4 oz/125 g) of the raspberries.
Combine the remaining raspberries and the sugar in a medium saucepan and cook over low heat until

RASPBERRY CREAM

1. Strain the raspberry purée through a fine sieve and stir in the gelatin.

3. Whip the cream until soft peaks form and fold in the remaining raspberry purée.

2. Pour 2 tablespoons of the raspberry purée into each of the molds and refrigerate for 30 minutes.

4. Pour the mixture over the raspberry gelatin and refrigerate for 30 minutes.

OPPOSITE: Raspberry Cream   PREVIOUS PAGE: Madeleines (left) and Caramelized Peaches with Vanilla Custard (right)

ABOVE: Strawberries in Raspberry Sauce

the sugar dissolves. Remove from the heat and let cool for 5 minutes.

Place the raspberry mixture in a food processor or blender and purée until smooth.

Strain through a fine sieve into a bowl and stir in the gelatin.

Divide the reserved raspberries between six 1-cup (8 fl oz/250 ml) pudding molds. Pour 2 tablespoons of the raspberry purée into each mold and refrigerate for 30 minutes.

Whip the cream until soft peaks form and fold in the remaining raspberry purée.

Pour the mixture over the raspberry gelatin (jelly) and cover with plastic wrap.

Refrigerate for 30 minutes, or until the cream feels firm to the touch.

Remove the plastic wrap and unmold onto plates and decorate with the extra raspberries.

Serve immediately.

STRAWBERRIES IN RASPBERRY SAUCE
Serves 4

¼ cup (1¾ oz/50 g) sugar
¼ cup (2 fl oz/60 ml) water
1 cup (8 oz/250 g) raspberries
1 lb (500 g) fresh strawberries
Heavy (double) cream, for serving
Lime zest (rind) julienned, for serving

Combine the sugar and water in a saucepan and stir over low heat to dissolve the sugar. Bring the mixture to a boil and boil for 2 minutes. Remove from the heat and set aside.

Process the raspberries to a purée. Strain through a fine sieve and stir in the sugar syrup. Hull the strawberries and serve them with the raspberry sauce and cream, and garnished with lime zest (rind).

ABOVE: *Bananas in Cointreau Caramel*

BANANAS IN COINTREAU CARAMEL
Serves 4

¾ cup (5½ oz/170 g)
packed brown sugar
¾ cup (6 fl oz/185 ml)
light (single) cream
10 tablespoons (5 oz/155 g)
sweet (unsalted) butter
2 tablespoons Cointreau liqueur
4 bananas, sliced
½ cup (1¾ oz/50 g) pecans, chopped
Plain yogurt, for serving

Combine the brown sugar, cream and butter in a saucepan. Stir over low heat until the sugar dissolves. Bring to a boil, reduce the heat and simmer, stirring, for 3 minutes. Remove from heat and whisk in the Cointreau. Add the bananas and gently stir until they are coated.

Divide among individual serving bowls and sprinkle with the chopped pecans. Serve with yogurt.

•

WHISKEY ORANGES
Serves 4

4 oranges
1½ cups (12 fl oz/375 ml) water
¾ cup (5 oz/155 g) sugar
⅓ cup (2½ fl oz/75 ml) Scotch whiskey

With a sharp knife, peel the oranges, removing as much pith as possible. Slice, or cut into segments. Combine the water and sugar in a saucepan and stir over low heat to dissolve the sugar. Bring the

mixture to a boil and boil until golden, about 5 minutes. Remove from the heat and stir in the whiskey. If the caramel hardens, return to low heat to dissolve. Place the peeled orange slices or segments in a serving bowl or in individual bowls and pour the whiskey sauce over them.
Serve immediately.

•

CITRUS TART
Serves 8–10

PASTRY
2¾ cups (10 oz/315 g)
all-purpose (plain) flour
13 tablespoons (6½ oz/200 g)
sweet (unsalted) butter
½ cup (3½ oz/100 g) sugar
1 egg

FILLING
Grated zest (rind) and juice of 3 lemons

1½ cups (10 oz/315 g) sugar
3 eggs
7 tablespoons (3½ oz/100 g)
sweet (unsalted) butter, melted
Confectioners' (icing) sugar
for decoration

Preheat oven to 350°F (180°C/Gas 4).
Pastry: Place all pastry ingredients in a food processor and process, pulsing, until the mixture just comes together. Press the mixture into a 12-inch (30 cm) springform pan. Prick the base with a fork. Bake for 10 minutes.
Filling: Place the lemon zest (rind), sugar and eggs in a food processor and process until the mixture is pale and creamy. Add the melted butter and process to combine. Add the lemon juice and process. Pour the mixture into the tart shell. Bake until the tart is just set, but still a little wobbly, about 30 minutes. Allow to cool slightly. Remove the sides of the pan.
Dust with confectioners' (icing) sugar before serving.

ABOVE: *Whiskey Oranges* OPPOSITE: *Citrus Tart*

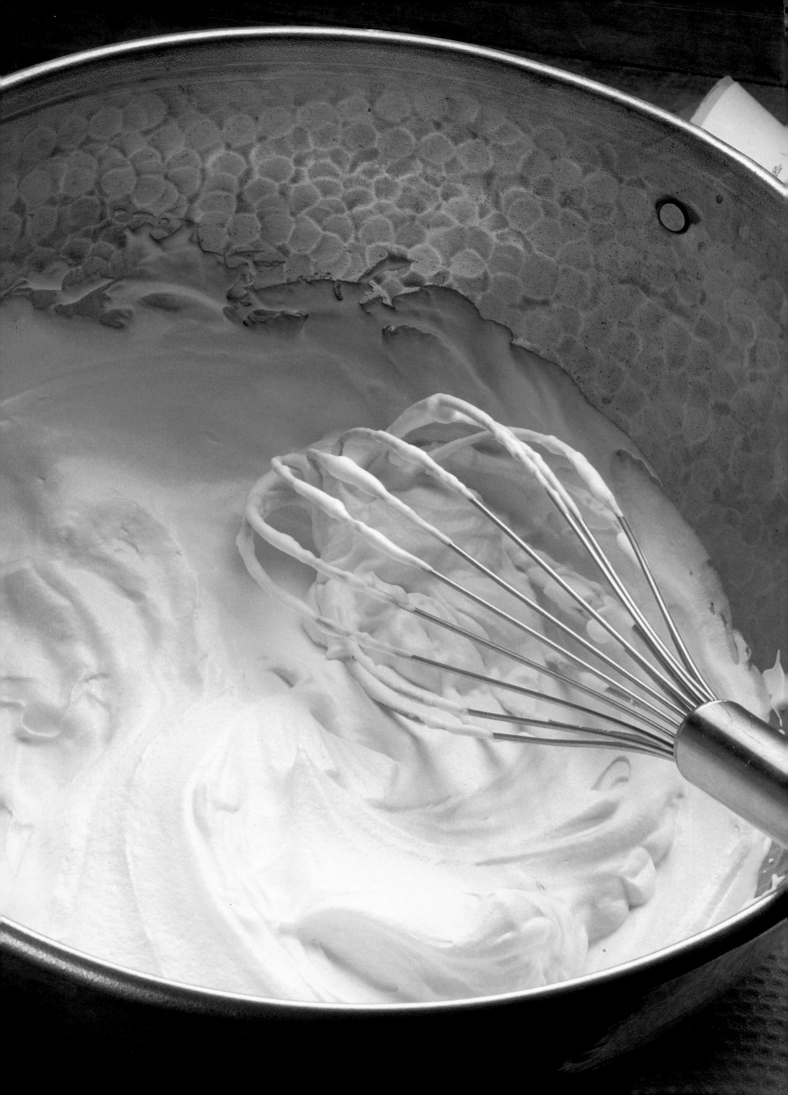

Accompaniments

·

Whether it is airy puff pastry or delicate swirls
of toffee, confident expertise gives the touch of
perfection and transforms a dessert from the
ordinary to the sublime. So, with a final flourish
of the baton, present your masterpiece
with aplomb and take a bow.

PUFF PASTRY

Makes 11 oz (345 g)

**2 cups (8 oz/250 g)
all-purpose (plain) flour
16 tablespoons (8 oz/250 g)
sweet (unsalted) butter, at
room temperature
1 teaspoon lemon juice
½ cup (4 fl oz/125 ml) ice water**

Sift the flour into a bowl. Rub in 1 tablespoon (½ oz/15 g) of the butter.

Combine the lemon juice and water. Make a well in the center of the flour and pour in half of the liquid. Mix with a knife to combine. As the dough begins to form, gradually add the remaining liquid a tablespoon at a time until the dough forms a mass. Turn the dough onto a work surface that has been dusted with a little extra flour and knead for 2–3 minutes. Roll the dough into a 10-inch (25 cm) square to a thickness of about 1 inch (2.5 cm).

Press the butter with a rolling pin until it is pliable and shape it into a 3–4 inch (7–10 cm) square. Place it in the center of the dough and fold the dough over the butter to enclose it completely. Wrap in plastic wrap and refrigerate for 10–15 minutes.

Unwrap dough and place on a lightly floured surface with the fold side facing upward. Roll the dough out to form a 6 x 12 inch (15 x 30 cm) rectangle that is about 1 inch (2.5 cm) thick. Fold the dough in thirds lengthwise. Gently pinch the edges together to seal and rotate the pastry 90° so that one of the pinched edges is facing you. Roll out again to a 6 x 12 inch (15 x 30 cm) rectangle, fold in thirds lengthwise and pinch the edges together to seal. Wrap in plastic wrap and refrigerate for 15 minutes.

Repeat the rolling until you have rotated the dough 6 times, refrigerating every other time. Refrigerate pastry until needed.

This puff pastry can be kept for 3 days in a refrigerator, or up to 1 month in the freezer.

An essential part of many desserts, puff pastry can also be rolled out, cut into shapes, brushed with a little beaten egg and sprinkled with sugar. These shapes are baked on a buttered baking sheet at 350°F (180°C/Gas 4) for 15–20 minutes, until puffed and golden. The shapes can be served as a crisp accompaniment to your dessert.

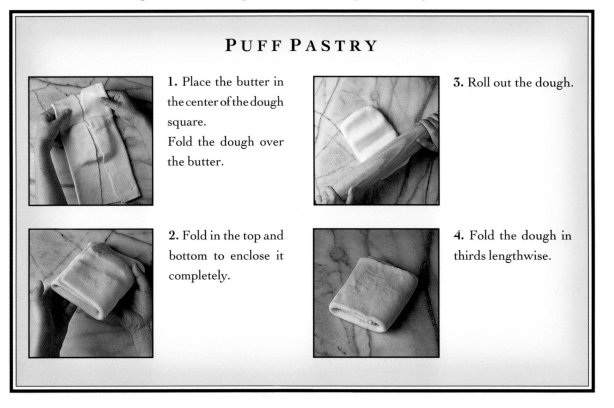

PUFF PASTRY

1. Place the butter in the center of the dough square.
Fold the dough over the butter.

2. Fold in the top and bottom to enclose it completely.

3. Roll out the dough.

4. Fold the dough in thirds lengthwise.

SPICED WHIPPED CREAM

Makes 1½ cups (12 fl oz/375 ml)

**1 cup (8 fl oz/250 ml)
heavy (double) cream
½ teaspoon ground cinnamon,
ground allspice, ground cardamom
or freshly grated nutmeg**

Whip the cream until soft peaks form. Stir in the preferred spice, adding enough to taste.

•

VANILLA ICE CREAM

Makes 3 cups (24 fl oz/750 ml)

**1 cup (8 fl oz/250 ml) milk
1 cup (8 fl oz/250 ml)
heavy (double) cream
2 egg yolks
¼ cup (1¾ oz/50 g) sugar
2 teaspoons vanilla extract (essence) or
seeds from 1 vanilla pod**

Combine the milk and cream in a saucepan and bring to boiling point. Remove from heat and add the vanilla.

Whisk together the egg yolks and sugar. Gradually whisk in the milk mixture. Return the mixture to a saucepan and cook over low heat for about 5–7 minutes, whisking gently, until the mixture thickens. Let cool before freezing in an ice cream machine, according to manufacturer's instructions.

•

BRANDY BUTTER

Makes about 1 cup (8 fl oz/250 ml)

**8 tablespoons (4 oz/125 g)
sweet (unsalted) butter
½ cup (3½ oz/100 g) sugar
2–3 tablespoons brandy**

Cream the butter until light and fluffy, adding the sugar a tablespoon at a time. Beat until pale then beat in the brandy. Spoon into a serving dish and refrigerate until hard.

Serve with Christmas or other fruit puddings.

TOFFEE SWIRLS

1. Combine 1 cup (6½ oz/200 g) sugar and 1 cup (8 fl oz/250 ml) water in a saucepan and stir over low heat to dissolve the sugar.

2. Bring to a boil and boil until golden, about 5 minutes.

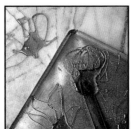

3. Working quickly, pour 1 tablespoon of the syrup onto a lightly oiled baking tray, swirling the spoon to get a "spider web" effect.

4. Allow to set until hard (about 5 minutes) before gently removing from the tray.

CRÈME FRAÎCHE
Makes 1½ cups (12 fl oz/375 ml)

**1¼ cups (10 fl oz/315 ml)
heavy (double) cream
2 tablespoons buttermilk**

Combine the cream and buttermilk in a screwtop jar. Cover tightly and shake for 1 minute. Let the jar stand at room temperature for 6–9 hours until the mixture becomes thick. Refrigerate to chill before serving.

•

RASPBERRY COULIS
Makes 1½ cups (12 fl oz/750 ml)

**1 cup (8 oz/250 g)
fresh or frozen raspberries
¼ cup (1¾ oz/50 g) sugar
1 tablespoon fruit-flavored liqueur**

Combine the raspberries and sugar in a food processor. Process to a purée. Taste and add more sugar if necessary.

Strain the purée through a wire sieve to remove the seeds. If desired, add 1 tablespoon of fruit-flavored liqueur.

This coulis can be used as a sauce with fruit or chocolate desserts.

ALMOND TUILES
Makes 36

**3 tablespoons (1½ oz/45 g) sweet
(unsalted) butter
⅓ cup (2 oz/60 g) sugar
Pinch of salt
3 egg whites
5 tablespoons all-purpose (plain) flour
½ cup (2 oz/60 g) sliced (flaked) almonds**

Preheat oven to 400°F (200°C/Gas 6). Butter 2 baking trays.

Cream together the butter and sugar. Beat in the salt and egg whites and beat until light and fluffy, about 3 minutes. Stir in the flour.

Drop teaspoons of batter onto the prepared trays, at least 4 inches (10 cm) apart. Using the back of a spoon, flatten the spoonfuls of batter so that they are 2 inches (5 cm) in diameter. Sprinkle each with a few of the almonds.

Bake the tuiles until the edges are just brown, about 5 minutes. Remove from oven. Using a spatula, turn tuiles over and bake for another 2–3 minutes. Remove from the oven and when still soft, mold the cookies over a rolling pin to get a curved shape.

These can be served with fruit or cream desserts.

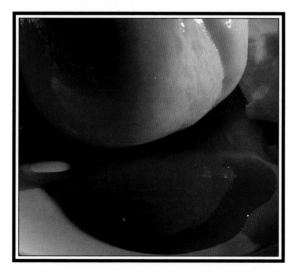

LEMON CURD
Makes about 3 cups (24 fl oz/375 ml)

4 lemons
12 tablespoons (6 oz/185 g) sweet
(unsalted) butter
2 cups (13 oz/410 g) sugar
4 eggs

Finely grate zest (rind) of the lemons and then squeeze their juice.

Melt the butter and sugar in a double boiler. Stir until smooth, do not allow to boil. Add the lemon zest and juice.

Beat the eggs together and then gradually whisk them into the lemon mixture over very low heat until the mixture thickens, about 5–7 minutes.

Pour into sterilized jars (10 oz/315 g). Allow to cool and seal.

The Lemon Curd is best eaten within 1 month of making.

•

BRANDY SNAPS
Makes 24

3 tablespoons light corn (golden) syrup
6 tablespoons (3 oz/90 g) sweet
(unsalted) butter
⅓ cup (2 oz/60 g) packed brown sugar
⅓ cup (1½ oz/45 g) all-purpose (plain)
flour, sifted
1 teaspoon ground ginger

Preheat oven to 350°F (180°C/Gas 4). Lightly butter 2 baking trays.

Place the syrup, butter and brown sugar into a saucepan and stir over low heat until the butter has melted. Remove from the heat and stir in the flour and ginger.

Drop teaspoonfuls of mixture onto the prepared trays, at least 3–4 inches (7–10 cm) apart. Bake for 5 minutes then remove from oven. Remove the Brandy Snaps from the tray and allow to cool for 1 minute. Gently roll each snap around the handle of a wooden spoon. Allow to cool on the handle for 2–3 minutes.

Brandy Snaps can be served either filled with whipped cream, or as accompaniments to ice cream.

ALMOND CREAM
Makes 2 cups (16 fl oz/500 ml)

½ cup (3 oz/90 g) almonds, toasted
3 egg yolks
3 tablespoons sugar
1 cup (8 fl oz/250 ml)
heavy (double) cream, whipped
2 tablespoons brandy

Place the almonds in a food processor and process to a fine meal.

Combine the eggs and sugar in a bowl and whisk until pale and creamy. Fold in the cream, brandy and then the almonds. Serve immediately.

Index

ACKNOWLEDGMENTS
Waterford Wedgewood